ANOTHER
SIX ENGLISH
TOWNS

ANOTHER SIX ENGLISH TOWNS

———

ALEC CLIFTON-TAYLOR

———

BRITISH BROADCASTING

CORPORATION

Published by the
British Broadcasting Corporation
35 Marylebone High Street
London W1M 4AA

ISBN 0 563 20215 7

First published 1984
© Alec Clifton-Taylor 1984

Printed in England by
BAS Printers Limited
Over Wallop, Stockbridge, Hampshire

CONTENTS

FOR

BRUCE NORMAN

SPONSOR AND FRIEND

WHOSE PASSION FOR ARCHITECTURE

HAS STOOD ME

IN SUCH GOOD STEAD

INTRODUCTION

Once again it is to a series of television programmes – produced this time not by Denis Moriarty but by Jane Coles, but with Bruce Norman again as Executive Producer – that this book owes its origin. Yet, as I observed last time, a set of television scripts and a book are very different. Not only is the book a good deal longer, but some of the sequences which seemed right for television have now been omitted.

The task of selection was as difficult as ever, for one can never come to the end of England! In 1976 I made a list of forty-six medium-sized or small towns which might, I felt, qualify for a television programme. To this four more were later added, making a total of fifty. With this, my third and probably last series, I have still only netted eighteen.

The present six were chosen, like their predecessors and only after lengthy deliberation, for their variety. They are neither better nor worse than the first twelve: just different. For instance, I have not hitherto included any town on the coast (although Berwick-upon-Tweed is very near). Now there is one: Whitby. Nor have I previously had a town with a major cathedral (although I have had Chichester). Now I have one: Durham.

Durham may not approve of being described as a town, for is it not a city? This prompts the interesting question: what makes a city? In the outback of the United States I have seen this term applied to places with no more than a gas station, a pull-up for hamburgers and a dozen shacks. In Britain the answer used to be quite simple: a town possessing an Anglican cathedral. Thus even St David's, which, in Findlay Muirhead's words, is no more than 'a somewhat straggling village on a treeless wind-swept plateau', is also, to quote the same author, 'the smallest "cathedral city" in the Kingdom'.

Since Victorian times, however, this definition has been modified. The term 'city', which is one of historical and ceremonial rather than of administrative significance (the first citizen being described as 'The Right Worshipful the Mayor' rather than simply as 'The Worshipful . . .'!), has been conferred by royal authority on important boroughs with no Anglican cathedral, such as Leeds, Nottingham and Cambridge. *Per contra*, every cathedral town is not now called a city. Southwell Minster was created a cathedral in 1884, but to hear the little Nottinghamshire town called a city would be, at the least, unusual; nor are St David's and St Asaph any longer so described. What then of Durham, Wells and Ely? Some of their citizens would, no doubt, vociferously defend their claims to reside in a city, and I would certainly not wish to break a lance with them over that. All have wonderful cathedrals; but Ely and Wells are in fact small country towns. Durham is larger, and looks much more magisterial: yes, Durham is indubitably a city. But for the purpose of this book it is also a town.

This time the selected towns vary appreciably in size. According to the last census (1981), Bury St Edmunds had 28,914 people, Durham 26,422, Cirencester 15,622, Whitby 13,763, Devizes 10,629 and Sandwich only 4227. But the larger places have outlying areas of which no account could be taken here. This is of no consequence architecturally.

All the towns described in this book have benefited from grants for repairs to their historic buildings. Until 31 March 1984 these were made by the Secretary of State for the Environment on the advice of the Historic Buildings Council. Since 1 April authority has been vested in the new Historic Buildings and Monuments Commission. The project was launched in 1953 as a result of the Report of the Treasury Committee on Houses of Outstanding Historic or Architectural Interest, appointed by Sir Stafford Cripps in 1948, and now generally known as the Gowers Report, after Sir Ernest Gowers, its chairman. All secular buildings listed as of outstanding architectural or historic interest became eligible for grants. Outstanding parish churches used for regular worship, including equivalent Nonconformist and Roman Catholic buildings but still exclusive of cathedrals, qualified in 1977.

Resulting from the Local Authorities (Historic Buildings) Act of 1962, and much aided by the Civic Amenities Act of 1967, under which it first became possible for Town Councils to designate Conservation Areas, another idea was developed: that of the Town Scheme, as it soon came to be called. This was, and is, a joint undertaking of the local authorities (Town Council, District Council or County Council, or any two of these, or even all three, as at Sandwich) and the Secretary of State, or, since 1 April 1984, the Historic Buildings and Monuments Commission. Within the terms of reference of the Town Scheme, which are (a) that the buildings must be within a Conservation Area and (b) that they must be of architectural or historic interest – although they need not be listed, since within Conservation Areas group value is also very important – grants are usually made on the basis of fifty per cent of the total cost of repairs, twenty-five per cent being paid by the local authorities and twenty-five per cent by the State.

At first this project moved very slowly. In 1970–1 there were still only twenty-five Town Schemes in operation. But since then it has steadily gathered momentum, so that by March 1983 there were 160, while by this date 2051 churches and chapels were in receipt of grants (about 2400 by March 1984).

All these six towns have Schemes except Cirencester, which had one from 1971 to 1976 from which it derived great benefit; it was then decided that the grants in this area should be diverted to other Cotswold towns (such as

Tetbury). The size of the grants varies; at Bury St Edmunds it is modest, but at all the other four it is at present between £20,000 and £30,000 a year. In every case, the grants have made a most valuable contribution to the town's improved appearance.

The range of the candidates for assistance continues to broaden. At Cirencester grants were made for paving and landscaping the West Market Place; at Durham for repairing the passageways known there as vennels. Elsewhere, help has been given for the renovation of gardens and for the repair of garden buildings. All this is indicative of the happy truth that our country is at last becoming ever more preservation-conscious. Thank goodness, philistine 'developers' can no longer count on having things all their own way.

In preparing the programmes for presentation on television, Jane Coles and I received much kindness and help from residents and officials in all the towns in which we worked, and I should like to record my warm thanks for all their willing co-operation, from which this book has likewise profited. I am indebted to Jennifer Jenkins and John Cornforth for detailed information about the Town Schemes and for other help relating to the Historic Buildings Council. Both were members, as they now are of the Historic Buildings Advisory Committee, under the Historic Buildings and Monuments Commission; Mrs Jenkins is again the chairman. In addition, special thanks are due to Kenneth Povah and Michael Colborne Brown for having each read and corrected the chapters devoted to their own town, and still more to Robert Storrar, for having read the whole book in typescript. As before, I owe a great debt of gratitude to Tony Kingsford, Books Editor of BBC Publications, to Peter Campbell, who for the third time has edited my book, and to Geoff Howard, who has once again taken almost all the photographs.

All the photographs in this book were taken by Geoff Howard except the following: Pages 15, 20 (top), Corinium Museum, Cirencester; 151, Bob Naylor, Chirton; 161, Country Life; 162 (left), The Kennet & Avon Canal Trust; 196, BBC Hulton Picture Library; 201, Brian Shuel; front cover, Airviews (M/c) Limited.

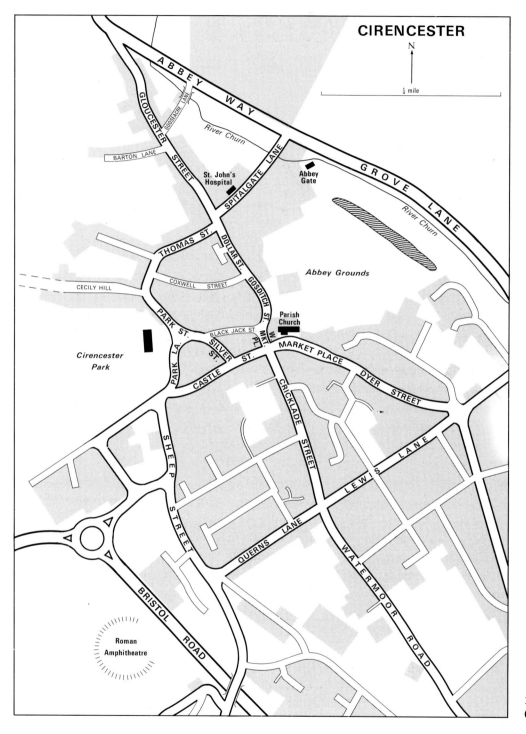

CIRENCESTER

N

¼ mile

ABBEY WAY

GLOUCESTER STREET

GOOSEACRE LANE

BARTON LANE

River Churn

SPITALGATE LANE

St. John's Hospital

Abbey Gate

GROVE LANE

River Churn

THOMAS ST.

DOLLAR ST.

GOSDITCH ST.

CECILY HILL

COXWELL STREET

Abbey Grounds

PARK ST.

PARK LA.

BLACK JACK ST.

Parish Church

MKT.

SILVER ST.

W. PL.

Cirencester Park

CASTLE ST.

CRICKLADE STREET

MARKET PLACE

DYER STREET

SHEEP STREET

LEWIS LANE

QUERNS LANE

WATERMOOR ROAD

BRISTOL ROAD

Roman Amphitheatre

1. *Plan of Cirencester*

CIRENCESTER

England possesses such a galaxy of small towns of high architectural quality that, although this is my third sextet, I have not yet been to the Cotswolds. This is surprising, for if I wanted to introduce a friend from abroad to English traditional architecture at its most *succulent*, it is there that I would take him before anywhere else.

The Cotswolds are a range of Jurassic limestone hills running from near Bath north and south-east through the whole length of Gloucestershire, spilling over into parts of Wiltshire, Oxfordshire and a small corner of Worcestershire, until finally dropping into southern Warwickshire. On the tops, the scenery is not beguiling; William Cobbett, who rode from Swindon across the Cotswolds to Gloucester on one of his Rural Rides in the 1820s, found it very much the reverse. 'I have never before', he wrote, 'seen anything so ugly. The stone lies very near to the surface. The plough is continually bringing it up.' So instead of hedges there were dry-stone walls, and very little woodland; and, although it was excellent country for sheep, he found it very cheerless, and greeted the fertile Vale of Gloucester with undisguised relief. But Cobbett was notoriously difficult to please. For many of us dry-stone walls – built, that is, without any mortar – are a continual delight. I am told that from one of the large cities in the North mindless idiots are prone to sally forth on their motor cycles to points where they find it very 'amusing' to push over and destroy what was built with so much skill and love: yet in our stone districts countless hundreds of miles of these walls happily survive.

In the Cotswolds, however, the visual pleasures belong to the valleys, and even there the scenery plays second fiddle to the architecture. Thanks largely to the local stone, it is the villages and farms which charm us most. Over and over again in this part of England, it is the buildings that steal the picture. That is equally true of the town widely acclaimed as 'the capital of the Cotswolds': Cirencester.

Of the six towns which form the subject of this book, Cirencester has easily the longest history: close on two thousand years. For here was sited the second largest town in Britain during the Roman occupation; only London was bigger. Today, at this place, as many as nine main roads converge; but what is of special significance is that no fewer than five of them are of Roman origin, with long stretches that are still straight for miles. Ermin Street comes in from the south-east and continues north-west to Gloucester. At what in Roman times

was the Forum this road crossed the Fosse Way, leading from Bath right across the Midlands to Lincoln. And diverging from the Fosse Way a mile to the north-east there was Akeman Street, which led eastwards to Bicester and ultimately to Colchester. (I use the past tense here because, although the route is known, this road has not survived nearly as well as the two others.)

The initial purpose of all these roads was, needless to say, military, and Cirencester, which in Roman times was known as Corinium, was in origin, like every Roman town in this island, a military settlement. The Romans had after all come here as conquerors; they were an invading army. But although some of the native chieftains, like Boudicca (Boadicea), put up a stiff resistance, others soon collaborated. There were no problems at Cirencester, which within a generation became a flourishing town; and so it remained for more than three centuries. It developed into a centre of local govenment, much more important than Gloucester, and a market for the agricultural produce of the many estates round about, and of the enveloping countryside. By the end of the second century it encompassed an area of about 240 acres (probably not all built over) and was surrounded by earthworks – an earthen rampart and a ditch – some two miles in circumference. Later the rampart was faced with stone, of which remains of a rather pathetic stretch can still be seen on the east side of the town; but most of this revetment stood no chance of surviving the demands of later generations for a convenient source of building stone.

2. The remains of the Roman Amphitheatre

3. Corinthian Capital in the Corinium Museum

The town was laid out in the usual unimaginative but practical Roman fashion, on a grid plan, and one or two streets, Lewis Lane in particular, follow the line of their Roman predecessors. Yet it is not the abundance but the scarcity of visible Roman remains which chiefly strikes us here today. The street pattern is of medieval, not of Roman origin, and a good job too, for the somewhat winding and often narrow medieval streets are visually much more rewarding. Outside the line of the Roman defences, a hundred yards or so to the south-west, can still be seen the remains of the Amphitheatre (plate 2), an earth construction whose large grassy slopes are now rather amorphous yet still quite impressive. The ring of seats rose in tiers some twenty-five feet above the central performing area. Of the external retaining walls of stone nothing survives.

Far more interesting, however, is the Corinium Museum, which has one of the best collections of Roman antiquities in Britain, and very well displayed. No visitor to Cirencester should fail to allow time for a visit. What other place in England but London could have yielded so imposing a piece of sculpture as the Corinthian Capital (3) dug up in two pieces in 1838? The huge leaves are of course that Roman favourite, the acanthus. The figures are more difficult to identify with certainty, but would all appear to be associated with Bacchus. On one face, it is believed, is the god himself, with his thyrsus or wand and a bunch of grapes, and on another his attendant, the demigod Silenus, with long hair and a drinking horn. The female figure illustrated would be one of the Maenads, priestesses of Bacchus. In her left hand she holds a tympanum or small drum.

What was the purpose of this big capital, which is $3\frac{1}{2}$ feet high? There is no evidence of its having been part of a building, and the current view is that it crowned a lofty column set up in some public place. Plate 4 shows a conjectural restoration. There is a dowel (shaped hole) on the top of the Capital into which could have been fitted the base of a pedestal for a statue. The bold, somewhat coarse style of the carving, which is in the local white limestone, is perfectly appropriate to an elevated situation.

For private citizens, the great status symbol in Roman Britain was a mosaic floor. Well-to-do people would have several of these in their houses. The Corinium Museum has a fine display, and they are still constantly turning up. Two have been found since 1970: the Hare mosaic (5) was discovered on an allotment in 1971. The animal occupying the central roundel is admirably rendered.

This hare has a few cubes of clear glass along its back, which in England is unusual. Almost all the materials employed for the mosaics were stone: little cubes, about half an inch square, known as tesserae, laboriously cut from a variety of different kinds, according to whatever colours were needed. The local Cotswold limestones were good for creams, yellows and greys. Blue-greys were obtained from the blue Lias limestone of the Severn Valley. Browns were of

4 (right). *Drawing showing conjectural siting of the Corinthian Capital*

5 (far right). *The Hare mosaic*

6 (right). *The Hunting Dogs mosaic*

sandstone, probably from the Forest of Dean. For dark greens and dull reds they used Purbeck marble. Brighter reds were obtained by firing clay, as with bricks and tiles. All these tesserae were carefully bedded into damp cement, and finally rolled and polished. They are exceedingly durable.

But this was essentially a Southern European art, and the craftsmen, some of whom were highly accomplished, must have come at the outset from the Mediterranean. Whether any native Britons were ever taught how to make mosaics is not known for certain, but seems probable.

The borders are designed with an interlocking pattern known as *guilloche*. The Romans were devoted to this form of ornamentation, and employed it everywhere: not only in England. Plenty of it can be seen in another of these floors, known as the Hunting Dogs mosaic (6). Marine monsters fill two of the half-roundels, but the central one has three dogs, full of life; unluckily their quarry, perhaps a stag, has disappeared. This floor, which dates from the second century, was found as long ago as 1849, and so was another one here, the Four Seasons mosaic, personified by female deities, with the Seasons now reduced to three, since Winter has been lost. This also belongs to the second century; but some of the largest and finest floors were not laid until two centuries later. From Barton Farm in Cirencester Park came a big mosaic floor of the fourth century, which has as its theme Orpheus with his lyre charming the animals and birds, represented in concentric circles around him: a subject which is also to be found at nearby Woodchester. The latest addition to the Museum's display is the Kingscote mosaic, which was only uncovered in 1975; the subject is believed to be Venus holding a mirror. It is a pity that not one of these mosaic floors is complete, but it is remarkable, surely, after nearly two thousand years, to have so much.

The Roman conquest conferred many benefits upon the country, of which no doubt the greatest was a long period of peace: the famous *Pax Romana*. At Corinium the summit of prosperity was not reached until the fourth century, when the population of the town was probably about 5000. The largest houses nearly all date from this time. In recent years a great deal of excavation has been undertaken, and this work continues.

Cirencester is on the Churn, a modest tributary of the Upper Thames (7), and that explains its name. 'Churn' was originally 'Coryn', hence the Roman name Corinium. Cester, Chester and Caster all derive from the Roman word *Castrum*, meaning a fort or fortified town, thus the modern name Cirencester means 'the fortified town on the Churn'.

When Leland was writing in the time of Henry VIII, this had become shortened to Cicestre, and about 1725 Defoe wrote 'Cirencester, or Ciciter for brevity,' while a century later Cobbett remarked: 'The people call it Cititer.' I recall the time when many people were still saying Ciceter or Cicester, but

7. Gooseacre Lane bridge over the Churn

hardly anybody does this any more: I am told, though, that many local people are still in the habit of calling the place just Ciren (which can sound rather like Zoiren!). And years ago I saw Ciren on more than one village signpost.

The Roman town was destroyed by the West Saxons in 577, and took a long time to recover. But the Danish invasion of the ninth century did not reach as far west, so it was a reasonably prosperous little town that fell to the Normans.

After about 1120, far and away the most important building here was the Augustinian Abbey; yet of this even less survives today than of the Roman town. At the Dissolution, as in so many other English towns, the Abbey buildings, like the Roman walls, became a convenient quarry for the new builders. If we keep our eyes open it is not difficult, now and again, to spot some of this pillaging. An example can be seen close by in Gloucester Street. No. 33 (8) is a timber-framed cottage erected on a fine plinth of beautifully masoned stone. No cottage would ever have had a plinth like this if the stone had not been there for the taking.

Above the ground, all that survives of the Abbey is the North Gate, dating originally from the twelfth century (10, 11). Both gates have a Norman arch of three orders, devoid of any carved enrichment; on the outer face there is

also a small postern gate. The walling is of local rubblestone, shaped to form level courses. The high-pitched, stone-slated roof looks no earlier than the seventeenth century. On its external face there is at present an excess of moss.

A few tantalising fragments of excavated medieval sculpture can be seen in the Museum. Of two women's heads unfortunately no records exist, so they cannot be ascribed to the Abbey with certainty, but I cannot resist illustrating one of them (9). Two smaller heads, of a pope and an abbot (12), may well have been portraits. But the site of this Abbey Church, which was half as long again as the present parish church although not as wide, is now no more than a vast lawn (13), the grounds of a demolished house which were for centuries private but which at last, in 1965, the local Council was able to purchase for the enjoyment of all.

In general there can be no doubt that the Abbey, which was very rich, was no friend of the town. From the time of Richard I the Abbot was lord of the manor. For several centuries these abbots were able to prevent the town from obtaining borough status and the privileges that went with it. Between the Abbey and the townspeople there was a recurrent feud. Today the lofty tower of St John's stands as a symbol of the townspeople's determination to be independent of the Abbey's authority. What happened was that on their own initiative they apprehended and summarily executed two rebel earls, half-brothers of the deposed Richard II. This so pleased the new king, Henry IV, that he

12. *Heads of a pope and an abbot in the Museum*

13. *The site of the Abbey, with St John's Church in the background*

rewarded the town with lavish gifts of money; the people responded by building the tower, and in the latest style, which was quite different from the thirteenth-century Early English nave.

Erected parallel with the Abbey church and just to the south of it, St John the Baptist was the town church. The tower (14) rises higher than any other parish church tower in Gloucestershire (162 ft), and is a striking feature in

14 (right). *The Church of St John the Baptist : tower and porch*

many views; but it has to be acknowledged that as a design it is not really a success. When it was started, about 1400, a spire was intended. But what the builders did not know was that this was the site of a filled-in ditch which had run along beside Ermin Street. So the foundations were not firm and the tower soon started to settle. Hence the very big buttresses, and also the awkwardness of the top. The projected spire (for which the supporting squinches can still be seen inside the clock storey) had to be abandoned, and instead they added, above the broad horizontal band which arrests the tower's verticality, a short top stage which is very obviously an afterthought.

The rest of the building, which is vast – it is the county's largest parish church, is a complicated amalgam, of several different dates. But the South Porch, one of the sights of England, was not under the control of the parish church until well into the eighteenth century. It was built about 1490, surprisingly, by the Abbey, whose lands all but surrounded St John's. It was originally an office building for the Austin Canons, and a very impressive one it must have been. Until the Dissolution, the Abbey controlled the market. Afterwards the porch became diocesan property, and from 1671 until 1897 this upper part

17 (right). *The fan-traceried vault in St Catherine's Chapel*

15 (far left). *The nave*
16. *The pulpit*

served as the Town Hall. The stone decayed and this part had to be rebuilt in 1831–3; when that happened the floor of the top storey, inside, was not replaced. But happily the exterior, with its profuse panelling and its oriel windows in triplets (14), remained unchanged. I know of no other parish church that has a porch three storeys high, nor one so sumptuous.

18 (far left). *St John's Hospital, Spitalgate Lane* 19. *Weavers Hall, 4–6 Thomas Street*

The old saying, which I cited when writing of Ludlow, that most of England's major parish churches were built on the backs of sheep, was certainly true of the Cotswold churches. On entering (15), the height of the arcades, the slenderness of the piers and the size of the windows all make an immediate impact. The church is very light, for it is a vast glasshouse: as good an example as can be found of Gothic structural ideas carried to their logical conclusion.

Perhaps the greatest delight is the fan-traceried vault, dating from 1508, over the long narrow chapel of St Catherine (17) to the north of the chancel. The masonry is beautifully crisp and sure. In view of the often bad relations between the Abbey and the town, it is good to note that this vault was in fact presented by one of the abbots.

A graceful feature of this church is the stone pulpit (16), of wine-glass form, dating from about 1450: one of the comparatively few pre-Reformation pulpits to have survived unscathed. There are also a number of excellent brasses, mostly of the fifteenth century, commemorating prosperous wool merchants. Reginald Spycer (d.1442) had four wives, William Prelatte (d. 1462) two; Robert Page (d.1434) had only one wife but she bore him six sons and eight daughters.

Another of the church's special treasures is the Boleyn cup, fully gilt and hall-marked 1535. This was presented in 1561, and is now exhibited in a special glass-fronted wall-case.

Little else survives from medieval Cirencester. There is a portion of the hall of what was once St John's Hospital (18), founded by Henry II, which has needed a good deal of restoration, but is still picturesque.

The oldest secular building, Weavers Hall (19), dating from the fifteenth century, is venerable rather than appealing. But *weavers* is a key word in the history of Cirencester. For the Cotswolds were, for many centuries, one of the great wool-producing areas of England. Today, despite much ploughing of pastures to grow cereals and vegetables, there are still about a quarter of a million sheep in this region, out of an English total of about twelve million. But most of them are now bred for mutton, which means not very high-quality wool. It has been estimated that in the fifteenth century England had about ten million sheep and the Cotswolds about half a million, including some of the special Cotswold breed with long, heavy fleeces, which were in great demand for warm clothing. Much of this wool was exported, the weaving being done in Flanders and elsewhere; but even in the twelfth century some cloth was made here, and the proportion earmarked for woven cloth gradually increased, partly because exports of raw wool became more and more heavily taxed.

By the end of the eighteenth century, the English wool trade had moved elsewhere, and the wealth of the Cotswolds was no longer dependent upon wool; but fine houses all over the town testify to the continuing prosperity of the clothiers and wool merchants throughout the seventeenth and much of the eighteenth centuries.

The focal point of the town is the Market Place, the shape of which is totally un-Roman. It is not specially large, and it is not regular. There is no hint of a formal square nor rectangle. The form is much more organic than that: and subtler (20).

The north side (21) is concave, and sweeps round in a gentle, continuous curve. The buildings, judging from their stucco fronts, mostly seem to belong to the eighteenth century. Moving eastwards from the church porch, we encounter a chorus of painted stucco. There are many colours, but, like the singing of a good choir, they blend harmoniously. The scale is right throughout. There could be no better example of the value of setting up a Conservation Area. What counts here is the group: not the individual buildings. Remove even one of them and it would be like extracting a front tooth.

These buildings are in fact by no means all equally old. Although their general aspect is Georgian, one or two are obviously Stuart, and behind their façades some are timber-framed and go back to the Tudor period. Only one has its frame exposed (22), and it does not take a moment to see how wrong that looks here – especially as what appear to be timbers have been ill-advised

21. *Market Place, north side*

blackened, while the plaster infilling is very white. Viewed close to, it is distressing to realise that what purport to be timbers are in fact mostly only painted stucco. Yet somebody must once have liked them, for some years ago the right-hand half of the Fleece Hotel, a very seemly Georgian building, was accorded the same treatment. The Civic Society, very active in this town, raised such an outcry that all this nonsense was, very properly, removed. One man was lucky. The fellow employed to paint on the bogus timbers was the very same man who was given the job of scrubbing them off again! What a pity that he was not able to deal with the other half in the same way, while he was about it. The Market Place would have greatly benefited.

The south side is convex, and a little more jerky; the buildings on this side are later, larger, more separate, and all stone-faced. And despite the usual expressionless sheet-glass windows, the winner for once is Victorian. The Corn Hall (23), of fawn-coloured Cotswold limestone of fine quality, and all ashlared, was built in 1862. There are carved masks on the keystones, and in the tympana over the first-floor windows (tympanum is the name given to the space between a lintel over a door or window and the arch above it) there are some delightful carvings by H. C. Frith (24).

The Market Place broadens as it moves westwards, but it has not always looked as it does now. This end belonged to the Abbot, who filled it with houses and shops; the names of the narrow streets, Butter Row, Butcher Row, Shoe Lane, indicated their trades. It was not until 1830 that these excrescent struc-

20 (left). *Market Place looking east*

22 (left). *Fleece Hotel, Market Place*

23 (right). *Corn Hall, Market Place*
24 (far right). *One of H. C. Frith's carvings on the Corn Hall*

tures were at last swept away. When this occurred the building line on the south side was brought forward about fifteen feet. Clustering around the west end of the church there were other houses, some built right up against the great porch and the tower. Later in the nineteenth century some of these were burnt; the rest did not finally disappear until shortly before the First World War.

This area, although not used for trading, is known as the West Market Place. Here stands the High Cross (25), a weather-worn medieval cross which rises from a square base enriched with Gothic tracery and a band of quatrefoils. In 1976, helped by an HBC grant, the surrounding space was attractively repaved and a few trees were planted: a great improvement.

The town still retains a generous sprinkling of later Stuart houses. Most of these preserve their casement windows. At 7 Black Jack Street (26) can also be seen hand-spun Crown glass, with its glinting reflections. The best of these houses, like 51 Coxwell Street (27), are ashlared throughout. The stone window-frames, which project slightly, are beaded, and stand on what are known as bullnose sills (28). It is a pity that the original leaded lights have been removed from some of the windows on the ground floor. This big house is now divided into flats. It evidently provided the model for the Rebecca Powell School in Gloucester Street (29). Although this was not built until 1740, the windows were never sashed. Again it is only on the first floor that they keep their original leaded panes. But the stone-slated Cotswold roof is attractive: there are seven

25 (right). *The High Cross*
26 (far right). *7 Black Jack Street*

27 (far left). *51 Coxwell Street, from a drawing by D. Wilkinson*

dormers to light the attic rooms. The narrow side wall of this building, at right angles to the street, is an enjoyable oddity: both the doorway and the window above are set within large, assertive, rusticated frames, decidedly rhetorical in character.

One of the most interesting seventeenth-century houses in Cirencester is Dunstall House, 27 Park Street (30). The front evidently yearns to be Georgian, but, equally clearly, is not. The proportions of the windows, with their moulded stone architraves, are obviously not Georgian, and the present glazing dates only from quite late in the eighteenth century; whether this replaced sash-framed windows with thicker glazing bars cannot be known, but the original windows were certainly casements with leaded lights. The coarse rubblestone walling of this front was intended to be rendered, and should perhaps still be; at present it is too rustic-looking for so important a site. The string courses do not correspond with the floors of the rather low rooms; no harm in that, but the point is worth observing. Excellent features are the doorway and the strong quoins.

28 (far left). *51 Coxwell Street: detail*
29 (left). *Rebecca Powell School, 3–5 Gloucester Street*

Within, this is a largely unspoilt Stuart house. There is nothing in the least Georgian about the oak staircase (31), with Ionic capitals crowning the flat balusters. Beyond is a room with exceptionally pretty and somewhat unusual panelling (32). It is apparent that already in the seventeenth century these wool merchants were sparing no expense in the adornment of their homes.

Back in Coxwell Street is a house which is historically perhaps the most memorable in the town. No. 53, now appropriately called Woolgatherers, still

30 (far left). *Dunstall House, 27 Park Street*
31 (left). *Dunstall House, Staircase*

32 (right). *Dunstall House, Dining Room*

33 (left).
*Woolgatherers, 53
Coxwell Street*

displays, well preserved, the whole story of the wool merchants. The central part (33) is the residence, built, like Dunstall House, of coursed rubblestone which, whether carried out or not, must have been intended to carry external rendering. Only on the second floor do the windows retain their original character, and even here the leaded lights are now larger than they would have been in the seventeenth century. On the first floor the windows have been sadly ill-treated. On the ground floor they have been sashed, and would look well if the glazing bars had not been mismanaged; an aperture of this shape demands three lights by five, not six. The stone doorcase, broad and somewhat low, carries conviction, and here the string courses do correspond to the interior floor levels. Within there are a Jacobean staircase and pleasing panelled rooms, not lofty, of the time of Queen Anne.

In front of the house, flanking wings frame a small courtyard. That on the left, connected somewhat clumsily with the main structure, is the former counting house, with its own entrance. Plate 33 shows the simple but pleasing handrail and the Cotswold stone roofing slates, delightfully restored and graded.

The right-hand wing is much higher, and on the far side, which looks on

34 (left).
*Woolgatherers,
from Thomas
Street*

35 (right). *12
Park Street*

36 (far left). *12 Cricklade Street*
37 (above). *14–16 Castle Street*

to Thomas Street (34), can be seen to form one end of a very different elevation (the other, built to balance it, has unfortunately been spoilt). Both these ends had, at first-floor level, Venetian windows, and between them, four storeys high, was the wool merchant's former warehouse. It is regrettable that most of the windows have been changed and a good many of them blocked, but this building is none the less a most interesting survival.

No. 12 Park Street (35) is another later Stuart house with a nice roof. As usual in the Cotswolds, the stone slates are rather small. The pedimented dormers still have diamond-shaped leaded lights in their casement windows: a very old-fashioned touch. Below, sash-frames were inserted, perhaps not until quite late in the eighteenth century: that at any rate is the date of the present windows. The walling is again only coursed rubblestone, which is now much in need of cleaning, but, unfortunately for these owners, rubblestone is today more expensive to clean than ashlar.

What a difference cleaning makes is well illustrated by No. 12 Cricklade Street (36). The fresh-looking cream-coloured Cotswold stone looks most engaging now. An unusual feature here is the carrying up into the eaves cornice of the architraves of the first-floor windows as lightly projecting panels.

Other examples of fairly recent cleaning can be seen in Dyer Street (38), where there is a string of big houses which are now nearly all offices. No. 5, with its Tuscan Doric portico, cannot have been built before 1800; this was formerly known as Wellesley House. No. 3, with the pediment, is somewhat

38. *3–5 Dyer Street*

earlier: a paradigm of quiet self-assurance. Both these houses have plat-bands to mark the storeys and continuous stone sills at first-floor level: in the case of No. 3 at second-floor level too. And every window is given character by means of delicately-wrought glazing bars.

These are the sort of houses which the Victorians dismissed as deadly dull, but fortunately the pendulum of taste has swung back again. Yes, with their fresh, smooth complexions and nicely washed faces, buildings like these can perhaps look a little bland, but reticence suits an urban street, and beautifully mannered they surely are.

The most striking, the most individual of all these Georgian houses is 14–16 Castle Street, which for nearly two hundred years has been occupied by a Bank (37). Built about 1720 by a wool merchant who was clearly *au fait* with the very latest fashion in architecture, this is Cirencester's one Palladian house; there was very little Palladian architecture anywhere in England as early as that. Set upon a rusticated stone plinth, the whole house was faced with the finest ashlar; but in the last fifty years the upper part has twice been given a coating of stucco, allegedly to counteract dampness; some limestones, admittedly, are inclined to be porous. In the 1930s great care was taken to match the colour of the stone exactly, but, as can be seen, it is now too white; the local Civic Society protested strongly about this at the time.

The proportion of window area to wall is quite different here from anything to be found elsewhere in Cirencester, and the front is exquisitely enriched by

39. *Cirencester House, yew hedge and Gateway*

details such as the balustraded panels below the first-floor windows and the small keystones in the guise of sculptured heads. Very satisfying, too, is the way in which the centre, under its pediment, breaks gently forward. The windows have obviously been changed. The Gothick tracery in the semi-circular heads of the six Venetian windows (so-called) is not, I feel, ideal, but the real misfortune is the Victorian plate glass on the ground floor. It is very much to be hoped that the missing glazing bars in these windows will be replaced.

Only a short distance from Lloyds Bank is one of the most extraordinary sights in England: a yew hedge said now to be forty-two feet high and twelve feet wide at the top; more at the base (40). This hedge, prefaced by a curious Gate-way (39) built of uncoursed rubblestone with rusticated ashlar quoins and a moulded cornice surmounted by three ball finials, effectively screens from the town its one mansion, Cirencester House.

This was built between 1714 and 1718 by the first Lord Bathurst on the site of an Elizabethan manor house, and his descendants have lived there ever since. At that time all the leading architects except Gibbs worked for the Whigs, who therefore got nearly all the best houses. Lord Bathurst was a Tory, and unfortunately he did not employ Gibbs, nor indeed any architect at all: just

40. *Cirencester House, the yew hedge*

the local mason. So the house, as he himself recognised, turned out to be decidedly plain (42).

Not so, though, the Park, which was what really interested him; he was primarily a plantsman, with a passion for trees. He was also a friend and patron of Alexander Pope, who gave him much help with the layout. The Park was laid out in the French manner with straight avenues converging on *rond points*. At one point no fewer than ten avenues meet. It was the last of the pre-landscape-gardening parks and one of the largest. The scale is immense.

From the west side of the house a wide avenue sweeps up to a Doric column carrying a statue of Queen Anne. This was not set up until 1741, when she had been dead for nearly thirty years. But it was an act of piety. Lord Bathurst's mother had been a close friend of the Queen, and it was to Anne that he owed his title.[1]

Far grander, however, is the Broad Avenue, which is not quite parallel with

[1] A barony, conferred in 1712. The first Lord Bathurst lived from 1684 to 1775. It was not until 1772 that he received, from George III, an earldom. 'To within a month of his death he rode two hours a day round his park, and drank, without fail, his bottle of claret or madeira after dinner.' (James Lees-Milne, *Earls of Creation* (1962), p. 55. This delightful book contains a detailed description of the making of Cirencester Park.)

the other, but also aligned on to the tower of St John's. This is fifty feet wide and stretches in a straight line for over four miles, nearly to Sapperton. But the first mile, seen in the photograph (43), was not planted until after the Earl's death. The trees flanking this splendid Ride are mainly beeches and horse chestnuts. With plenty of lime in the soil, beeches grow profusely around Cirencester. But Bathurst also planted oaks and elms in abundance, together with occasional yews and conifers. Some parts of the estate were already so well wooded that, in addition to planting, he also had to do some cutting down.

The Park is dotted with so-called 'Ornaments', such as Alfred's Hall, an early example of a castellated folly, and Ivy Lodge, which has a central tower and gabled ends. But for these some of the other Georgian parks are far more memorable. Its ten thousand acres are freely open to pedestrians, but not to wheeled traffic. The Georgian screen at the entrance, with its exquisite wrought-iron overthrow, is not easily forgotten, but it was only installed here in Victorian times.[1]

The approach to the gates is up Cecily Hill, the widest street in Cirencester, and, its residents would probably tell you, the town's best address (41). The architecture of the houses is, as generally in this town, a pleasure, but no more so, in my view, than in several other streets. What distinguishes Cecily Hill are its spaciousness, its gradient – for most Cirencester streets are flat – and the view up the great avenue at the far end. At its lower end the street contracts, which enhances the impression of its length. The best house, although not ashlar-faced, is No. 32 (44), with a pleasing doorcase, a bold, well-proportioned pediment and modillioned cornice, and original Crown glass in all the windows.

[1] It is frequently said that this screen came from Carshalton Park, but that is an error. The famous Carshalton Park screen and gates are now at Planting Fields, one of the great gardens of Long Island (see *Country Life*, 1 March 1984).

42 (right). *Cirencester House*

43 (right). *The Broad Avenue*

41. *Cecily Hill from the Park*

At the top end of Cecily Hill is Cirencester's most improbable building, a castellated structure of quite imposing proportions (45). Can it be another of the Park's 'Ornaments': the largest of them all? Not at all! Built in 1857, this was formerly the armoury of the Royal North Gloucestershire Militia. Hence the toy fort effect, with an array of battlements and a circular drum tower at the angle. The octagonal stair turret of the gatehouse is not only battlemented but machicolated. All the windows are lancets, but trefoil-headed. In accordance with Victorian architectural principles, the elevation is in every detail asymmetrical. It is well built and not unattractive. Its solid qualities make it a very suitable headquarters for the Town Band. It is also used commercially for storage.

44. *32 Cecily Hill*

Throughout the Victorian and Edwardian eras, however, when many English towns were expanding fast, Cirencester marked time. The cloth trade faded out, to be replaced by agriculture: corn, cattle, cheese-making. No trunk line came here, and for nearly twenty years now there has been no railway at all. Since it is eighteen miles from both Cheltenham and Gloucester, and still further from Swindon, it is very much a social entity of its own.

The historic town is tightly knit. It had to be, because it was wedged between two large estates, the former Abbey lands to the north-east and the Park to the west, which together acted as a strait-jacket. For many years it was only towards the south-east that expansion was possible.

Architecturally this was no misfortune. Cirencester escaped that rash of Victorian commercial and institutional buildings, and houses, mostly ugly, which marred so many English towns at this time. In 1911 the population was only 7632. Since then it has doubled. It still has considerable dependence on the surrounding countryside, including, nowadays, the supply and repair of agricultural machinery. But it also has an industrial estate, combining light engineering, electronics, printing and so on. It is the United Kingdom headquarters of a Japanese car importer, and is becoming increasingly a centre for computer activities.

In almost every direction, a little way off, there is now new housing, but it does not impinge upon the older streets. The whole of the historic town is a Conservation Area, and from 1971 to 1976, as mentioned in the introduction

45. *The Barracks, Cecily Hill*

(p. 8), reaped the benefits of a Town Scheme, administered by the Urban District Council, which in 1974 gave place to the Cotswold District Council.

A visit to the Council Offices is likely to provide a surprise, for they are based in the old Workhouse, built about 1840. After the Second World War this building became a hospital for geriatrics, which, needless to say, was visually no advantage to it. The conversion to Council Offices took place in 1979–80. The unsightly accretions were removed; a new entrance hall was added, with a small topknot (46). It could, and should, have been done less parsimoniously, but the decision to make this conversion, rather than to destroy the building and replace it by a new one which might well have been in a decidedly faceless style, was surely right, as well as being considerate to the ratepayers.

The visitor will quickly become aware of the small concrete blocks with interlocking wavy edges which now cover many of this town's pavements (47). They can be seen in other places too: at Gloucester, for example, and indeed here and there in London. At Cirencester many have been laid since 1979. They have a number of advantages over ordinary paving stones, besides their attractive appearance. If drivers of motor vehicles insist on parking on, or partly on, pavements, these new tiles do not crack so easily; they are set only in sand and are easily replaced. They have a nice echo of cobbles, and come in several different colours.

On the whole, planning here has been skilful. There is a ring road (or, to be quite accurate, three-quarters of a ring road) which takes much of the through traffic well away from the centre. Another excellent feature is the loca-

46. The Council Offices

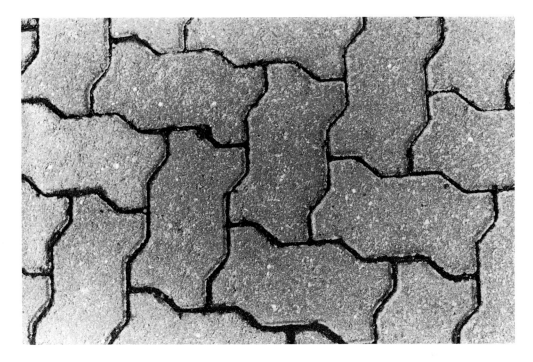

47. *New Paving*

tion of car parks. They are spacious and surprisingly central, yet every one of them is tucked away behind the street frontages, so that, whereas in other towns they are often eyesores, here they impinge visually very little. And none, thank goodness, is multi-storeyed.

So Cirencester is today very much 'a going concern' again, prosperous and enlightened. With a well-conducted District Council and, as mentioned earlier, a flourishing Civic Society, acting as a friendly watch-dog, the future prospects for this town look excellent.

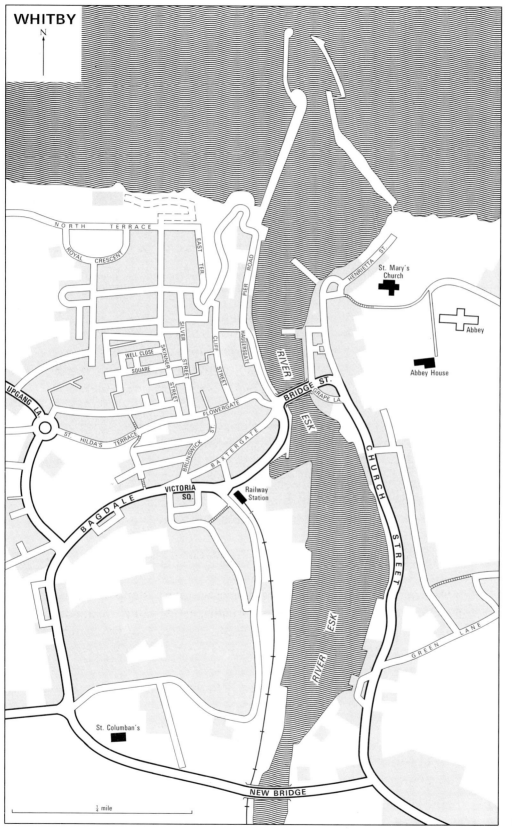

WHITBY

N

NORTH TERRACE

ROYAL CRESCENT

EAST TER.

PIER ROAD

SILVER STREET

WELL CLOSE SQUARE

SKINNER STREET

CLIFF STREET

HAGGERSGATE

FLOWERGATE

UPGANG LA.

ST. HILDA'S TERRACE

BRUNSWICK ST.

BAXTERGATE

BAGDALE

VICTORIA SQ.

Railway Station

RIVER ESK

BRIDGE ST.

GRAPE LA.

CHURCH STREET

Henrietta St.

St. Mary's Church

Abbey

Abbey House

GREEN LANE

St. Columban's

NEW BRIDGE

¼ mile

1. *Plan of Whitby*

WHITBY

Whitby, 24 July. This is a lovely place. The little river Esk runs through a deep valley which broadens out as it comes near the harbour. A great viaduct runs across with high piers, through which the view seems somehow further away than it actually is. The houses of the old town are all red-roofed, and seem piled up one over the other anyhow.... Right over the town is the ruin of the Abbey, a noble ruin of immense size. Between it and the town is another church, the Parish one, round which is a big graveyard, all full of tombstones. It descends so steeply over the harbour that part of the bank has fallen away, and some of the graves have been destroyed.

That is a passage from *Dracula*, the famous novel of horror and superstition by Bram Stoker, published in 1897. And the extraordinary fact is that his impression of Whitby remains almost as accurate today (2) as when the book first appeared. There can be very few English towns which have been able to retain their nineteenth-century character as completely as this one.

Many who have never been there will have heard of the Synod of Whitby, at which, in the year 664, Oswy, King of Northumbria, decided in favour of the Roman form of Christianity in preference to the Irish, a momentous decision for Britain. But the monastery which was the meeting place of the Synod, and which was founded in 657 by St Hilda of Hartlepool, was destroyed two centuries later (867) by the Danes, and not refounded until the coming of the Normans.

The present abbey church (3, 4) was probably started in the very same year as Salisbury Cathedral, 1220, and although so far apart, they have, stylistically, a good deal in common. There are the lancet windows, stepped up in the gable, the dog-tooth mouldings, the simple quadripartite vaults: hallmarks, all of them, of the Early English style, the first phase of our Gothic church architecture. In the nave (5) the middle phase, the Decorated, is also represented, by a pair of beautiful traceried windows (of which only one is seen in the photograph). But of any later date than the early fourteenth century there is nothing at all.

The monks belonged to the Benedictine order, and never numbered more than sixty. In December 1539 they departed, and their Abbey was abandoned to the wind and the rain and the pillagers of stone. Yet for over two hundred years the church, though unroofed, remained otherwise largely intact, and the central tower only fell in 1840.

One reason for this was the strength of the stone, which is Jurassic sandstone,

2. *Whitby from the new bridge*

taken from three different quarries in the vicinity. The best known by far is the sandy-brown stone from Aislaby. The quarries were above the north bank of the Esk, some four miles upstream from Whitby. The blocks were loaded on to carts, hauled probably by oxen, and taken down to the river. Then having been ferried across, they were dragged up the hill by the same means. Aislaby sandstone has been a great gift to the whole of this neighbourhood and it has travelled far beyond: even, in the eighteenth century, to build Houghton Hall in Norfolk.

To erect the Abbey, however, they also used a light-grey sandstone from Sneaton, which is closer to Whitby and with quarries above the right (south) bank of the river: the same side, that is, as the monastery itself. And finally the builders availed themselves of a dark-brown ironstone quarried on the cliff-top only two or three hundred yards away. These three stones, quite distinct, would seem to have been blended without any obvious method.

Before the Ministry of Works took over in 1920, the ruins, still privately owned, were totally neglected. A favourite pastime of the local youths was throwing stones up at the carved figures to try to knock off their heads; all too often they succeeded. And of course wind and rain have taken their toll. But on this highly exposed site the wonder is that so much has survived so well. This lovely, evocative ruin towers over Whitby and can be seen for miles, both inland from the moors and from the waters of the North Sea.

Opposite
Whitby Abbey
3 (top). *The east end*
4 (right). *From the west*
5 (far right). *From the south-west*

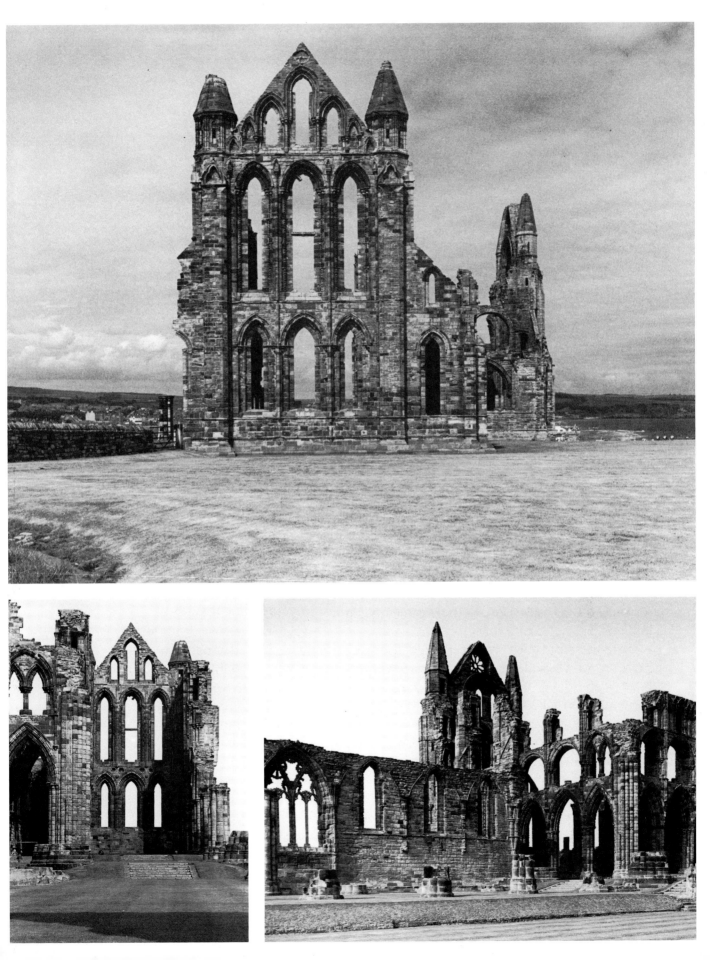

6. *Abbey House: the Banqueting Hall*

After the Dissolution, the Abbey and its land were bought by one Richard Cholmley, whose son Francis, at the time of the Spanish Armada, built a house. Abbey House, as seen today, is not Cholmley's. It is unashamedly Victorian, and now run as a holiday home. But masking it is a very odd building (6). In the time of Charles II another of the Cholmleys, Sir Hugh, built, with stone taken from the Abbey, a grand Banqueting Hall 210 feet long, with an imposing external centrepiece in a style verging on the Baroque. It is difficult to believe that it housed many banquets; for one thing, who would have come to this inaccessible, windswept spot? Less than a century later it was badly damaged in a gale, and soon after that the Cholmleys moved away for ever to another of their estates. Hence the blind windows of this roofless shell: not beautiful, but haunting, strange, almost eerie.

7. *St Mary's Church, from the south-west*

Only two other buildings occupy this cliff-top: a long range of cottages which is now a Youth Hostel, and St Mary's Church.

St Mary, as we see it today (7), is not of any great consequence as a work of architecture, with its big squat tower, several external staircases affording access to internal galleries, and a mainly Georgian north side which is really rather comical (8). But the interior is unforgettable. It is not a work of art, but a most illuminating social document. Here can be seen, as nowhere else in England, what the Georgians thought about a medieval church, and what they were prepared to do to it (10). That it should have emerged from the age of Victorian piety unscathed is little short of miraculous.

The best place from which to take it all in is the three-decker pulpit, a most endearing piece with a pretty, crested sounding-board, which until 1847 stood

8. *The north side*

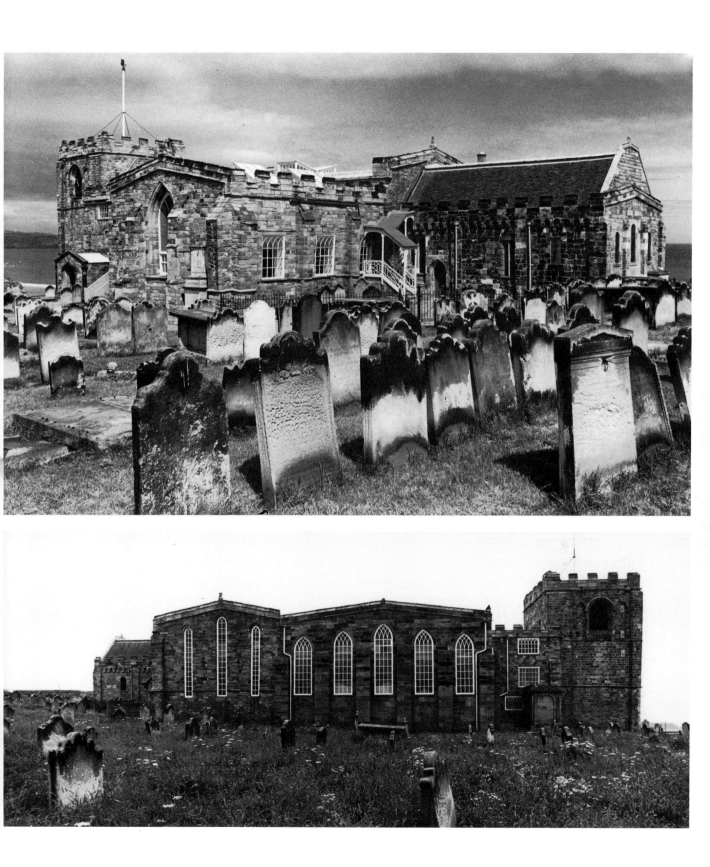

at the eastern end of the central aisle. Below a Norman chancel arch there was once a screen surmounted by a rood: the image of Christ crucified flanked by the Virgin Mary and St John. What occupies that place today is a family pew, supported on four barley-sugar posts (9). This, as some would say, blasphemous object was installed by the Cholmleys late in the seventeenth century. From time to time it is still occupied by a descendant.

9. *St Mary's: the Cholmley pew*

The galleries started to appear about 1697, as Whitby became more popular. They went on increasing until 1818, by which time the church could seat two thousand people, as it still can and occasionally does. The earliest pews, those with straight ends and two knobs, are Jacobean, but most are Georgian and extremely uncomfortable. Characteristically, some are painted white, others not. The outcome is a glorious jumble.

Of all England's parish churches, St Mary was for centuries one of the most arduous to reach; yet the people came crowding in. Now there is a circuitous driving road round the back. But before that was made the only approach was by the precipitous Donkey Track, which looks as if it climbs at about one in two, or by the famous steps (11). These, all 199 of them, belong to the Rector and Churchwardens, and their maintenance is a constant drain on church funds.

10. *St Mary's: interior and pulpit*

They too are of Aislaby sandstone, but originally they were made of wood.

Up these steps, for generation after generation, came not only the living, but ultimately, also, the dead. So when we look at such of the Georgian tomb-stones as have survived the rigours of the weather in this historic spot (12), it is well that we should remember that all the coffins of those commemorated had to be lugged up that dauntingly steep hill.

Who were these people? What did they do? Quite unlike the citizens of Cirencester and so many other English towns, they had nothing to do with sheep, nor wool. The prosperity of Whitby, which reached its peak during the eighteenth century, was based primarily upon the sea. Men of Whitby habitually went fishing, and especially whaling. Until the opening of the first turnpike road in 1759, access to this town was also usually by sea.

In the seventeenth and eighteenth centuries, shipbuilding and ship-repairing were important industries here. It was Whitby men who built the wooden ves-sels which carried Captain Cook, a local celebrity, on his great voyages of dis-covery. Almost all the wood for this activity was brought in from the Baltic or from Scandinavia.

There were also minerals. The chief were sandstone, quarried above the banks of the Esk, especially around Aislaby, and alum, mined near Guisborough. For both, the port of dispatch was Whitby. But the quarrymen

11. *The church steps*

and the alum miners did not live in Whitby. The mariners, the fishermen and the shipyard workers did. It was for them that the old town came into being; and, although shipbuilding here is no more, Whitby is still a fairly flourishing fishing port.

Some of the houses and cottages, especially in the vicinity of the harbour, are still occupied by fisherfolk. Timber-framing here is exceptional; the usual materials are either stone or brick. Nos. 20–22 Church Street (13), facing the harbour and dating from the eighteenth century, are typical. The blocks of sandstone are comparatively large. The roofs are pantiled. Some of the original windows have survived; others had been altered. No. 20, like many others here, has been rendered, perhaps for greater warmth. A little farther along Abbeville Cottage (14), flanked today by two modern houses, has been unkindly treated in various ways, but is a cosy little Georgian survivor. Whether of stone or brick, a good many of the cottages, when not rendered, have been whitewashed.

The Old Smuggler in Baxtergate (15) used to be an inn known as The Old Ship Launch. The doorway goes back to the fifteenth century. The windows are Georgian, and sash-framed, but instead of moving up and down, on cords, they slide sideways. With low rooms that was the only way. And because of

13 (far left).
*20–22 Church
Street*
14 (left).
*Abbeville Cottage,
37a Church Street*

their prevalence in this county, these are often known as Yorkshire windows.

The tooling of the surface of the stone blocks is better seen on other buildings in the town (16); Whitby can show many specimens, and very pleasing it is. So far as I am aware, it is hardly to be found except in the North-East, where it is quite common: a prime example, in fact, of what was a purely local develop-

15 (left). *The Old
Smuggler, 29
Baxtergate*

16 (right). *1
Wellington Road*

ment. It was done with a punch, a hammer-headed tool with a very narrow cutting edge. The mason worked from both the long edges of each block diagonally, to produce a V shape (17). The origin of this practice was probably economic. Dressing a block in this fashion did not take so long nor cost so much as producing an ashlared surface. The effect is rougher, but suits the locality very well.

What emphatically does not suit either the locality or the stone is the harsh pointing seen in plate 18. The joints which seem to have needed to be filled here were very wide, and much of the filling is at least tactfully coloured, but the centre of each joint is much too assertive and cementy-looking.

Many of these small properties are situated in what are known as the Yards, which are a feature of Whitby. Before about 1700 the typical house-plot was a long narrow strip, often stretching steeply uphill. When with increasing prosperity the population rose, many of these strips were sold off for additional housing, often accessible only by a passage running under a corner of the original house (20). It would be misleading to suggest that all the dwellings in these Yards were well equipped with mod. cons. Many had only outside lavatories; some still do. They could even be at some little distance from the house. But in recent years a good deal of tactful modernisation has been undertaken.

19 (right). *Pantiles near the Harbour*

17 (far left). *Herring-bone tooling, Hillside Cottage, McLacklin's Yard*

18 (below). *Pointing, Boltons Buildings, McLacklin's Yard*

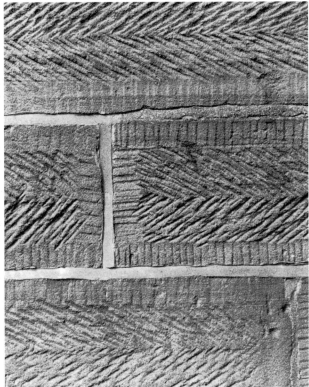

24 (above). *9–11 Upgang Lane*

25 (far right). *19 Grape Lane*

Opposite
20 (top left). *Elm Yard, Baxtergate*

21 (top right). *Salt Pan Well Steps*

22 (far left). *5 Wellclose Square*

23 (left). *44 Cliff Street*

To live in some of Whitby's houses, however, one does need to be something of a mountain goat. Salt Pan Well Steps (21) lead to a terrace not built until 1816, when land near the harbour had really become very scarce indeed. There are many other flights of steps on both flanks of the harbour. Climbing them generally brings at least one very agreeable reward: a pantile-scape (19). Whitby has large numbers of red pantiles, which make a delightful contribution to the town's colour and visual texture.

Much more unusual is another feature which occurs here to a greater extent than I have ever encountered elsewhere: the very long window. Five centuries before, it is true, York Minster had produced its 'Five Sisters', a quintet of lancet windows each five feet wide and fifty-three feet high; and here at Whitby it was also the parish church which, in 1744, led the way (8). But private houses soon took up the theme. At 5 Wellclose Square (22) there is a window only two lights wide but ten up. At 44 Cliff Street (23) the head of the window is arched, with Gothick tracery. This window is fixed; just one light is hinged and can be opened. Nos. 9 and 11 Upgang Lane (24) are a pair of late eighteenth-century houses, each dominated by an immensely tall window over the front door containing, including the five in the arch, no fewer than forty-one lights. Freakish they may be, but they are certainly fun! Much more fantastic, though, is the extraordinary 'bottle window' at 19 Grape Lane (25), in which the panes number in all sixty. This is perhaps the strangest window in any domestic building in the country. One is always cautious about employing the word unique, but I have certainly never seen another.

What now of Whitby's larger houses? Earlier than the end of the seventeenth century, about the only one to be seen, and that much restored, is Bagdale Old Hall (26), once the home of several noted local families. This is an L-shaped house built originally in the reign of Henry VIII, but not much of the original character has managed to survive.

Later, when the town was at last beginning to become prosperous, the most successful people, as so often, tended to move a little way out. Ruswarp Hall (now Old Hall Hotel), in the village of Ruswarp, a mile and a half to the southwest, is a late seventeenth-century house built of brownish-red brick with sand-

27 (right). *Ewe Cote Hall*

28 (right). *Larpool Hall*

26. *Bagdale Old Hall*

stone dressings. The windows have elaborate pediments and the building has character, although it has not, to put it mildly, been improved by the Welsh slate, Victorian dormers and mean additions to either side. Ewe Cote Hall (27), about the same distance to the west, is simpler but better preserved, although it is a pity that the red of its new pantiles is so shrill. Otherwise this stone house, which was built in 1697, gives pleasure and looks lovingly maintained. Larpool Hall (28), a mile to the south, is not lovable, and was marred in the Victorian period by the addition of a protruding porch and an ugly bay window with sheet glass, but stately it assuredly is. It was built in the 1780s, and entirely of the local sandstone. The masonry is excellent, and the site superb: it commands an immense prospect. Grander still was Sneaton Castle, close to Ewe Cote Hall. This is an early nineteenth-century mansion in the castellated style, also well sited, with its park. But it is now a school, and the front elevation is much marred by the proximity of a large new chapel.

Architecturally, the most interesting of these large houses on Whitby's periphery is St Columban's, which was built in 1790 for a wealthy shipowner, landowner, JP and local bigwig: it was formerly known as Airy Hill. The material is not, here, Whitby's Jurassic sandstone but the still more durable

29. St Columban's, north side

30. *St Columban's, south side*

Carboniferous sandstone with characteristic 'watermarkings', brought, no doubt at high cost, from the West Riding. The front elevation (29) is full of interest; the ground-floor windows have Gibbs surrounds (that is, architraves with large blocks arranged intermittently) and triple-stepped keystones, and the Victorians, here too, added a porch, but far more skilfully than at Larpool Hall: this one is a real embellishment to the house. Above the front door is a big Venetian window with Ionic columns and radiating rustication, set within a rusticated panel. In the pediment is an oval window with, again, a Gibbs surround. The garden front (30) is no less accomplished and still more original, especially in the elaborately-carved architrave of the central window on the first floor, which is *sui generis*. Equally unusual are the curved ramps at each end of the parapet, containing urns. The triple-stepped keystones of the ground-floor windows find an echo here in the frame of the bull's-eye window in the pediment. How sad it is that in both pediments the glazing of the windows has been altered so ineptly. But there is far worse to record than that. St Columban's has been extremely unlucky. With the construction a few years ago of a new by-pass road, it exchanged most of its garden for the noise of incessant traffic. It became a school, and then for several years stood empty and was vandalised. Essential repairs have now been carried out, but at the time of writing (early 1984) its future is uncertain.

Low Stakesby Mansion (32, 33) is another good house of the time of George III, formerly set in extensive grounds. It is now divided up into flats and surrounded by a housing estate. Here only the dressings are of stone; there are few of the subtleties of St Columban's, and once again a Victorian porch, which is visually no asset. But the red brickwork is of unusually high quality for Yorkshire, and impeccably pointed. The house is in good condition, and from the garden side, which was originally the entrance front, there is a wide view.

Closer to the town centre the handful of large Georgian houses, all on the west side of the river, are no longer residential (at least on their lower floors). Some, like the once stately house in Haggersgate that is now the Mission to Seamen, or the one in Flowergate which is now the Working Men's Club, have clearly known better days. When in 1870 the latter became the Crown Hotel, its Georgian front was brutally masked. Others, like 23 Baxtergate (34), have become offices and are well maintained, at any rate externally; this one, of sandstone, has a delicate dentillated cornice below the parapet, and, like most of these houses, has kept all its original glazing bars, so vital to its good appearance. 10 Brunswick Street, also now offices, has a good doorcase of the Tuscan order and, over the door, an unusual and very attractive honeysuckle fanlight (35).

In the later Georgian period, however, many Whitby people preferred to

32, 33 *Low Stakesby Mansion,* (right) *north front and* (far right) *south front*

31 (left). *1–3 Brunswick Terrace*

34 (right). *23 Baxtergate*
35 (far right). *10 Brunswick Street*

39 (above). *3–4 St Hilda's Terrace*

36 (top left). *12–14 Bagdale*

37 (far left). *24 St Hilda's Terrace*

38 (left). *19 Wellclose Square*

live in terraces; and towards the town centre it is these that are generally in much better shape today than the big detached houses. Brunswick Terrace (31) consists of three houses only, and the architecture, though endearing, is a trifle naïve. When I saw those flights of steps I thought 'Pity the poor postman', until I was relieved to find that there are also doors opening on to a high-level street at the back. Bagdale has kept a handsome range of houses, built from 1780 onwards, which do not exactly form a terrace, but Nos. 12 to 14 do (36); what a pity that some of the windows have been changed. Here the facing material is not brick but ashlared stonework, and all the architraves are enriched. The stone of this well-sited terrace would greatly benefit from cleaning.

St Hilda's Terrace is now, I suppose, the best address in Whitby. It has twenty-five houses, but again they do not form a continuous terrace. It is evident that, for better or worse, the development proceeded not as at Bath but as so often in London: the plots were sold off separately and each purchaser 'did his own thing'. So there is considerable diversity. No. 24 (37) is one of the largest and most enjoyable. All these houses have steep gardens in front and service entrances at the back. Some of them have doorcases of high quality.

41. *Whitby Piers and Lighthouses*

Nos. 3 and 4 (39) have fluted Ionic pilasters, dentillated pediments, pretty fanlights and six-panel doors in the absolutely correct proportions. Why *will* some people change their Georgian doors, invariably for the worse?

One of the pleasures, however, of strolling round the older parts of Whitby is looking at the doorways. The number of good ones that have survived is considerable. Often, as at 19 Wellclose Square (38), the base of the pediment is open, to allow room for the arch of the fanlight, which here is simple but very graceful. Turning to the surrounding wall, we can also see very clearly how, around 1800, cement rendering was regarded as no more than an economical substitute for stone. Hence the incised lines, made with a special jointing-tool, which were intended to suggest the mortar courses between ashlared stone blocks.

Pretty little fanlights may adorn even the most modest houses, like 44–45 Baxtergate (40), where the twin doors march in double harness under a single open pediment. The patchings here leave much to be desired, as also does the pointing, all of which is either too dark or too light; but at least the facing material is all stone: ashlar, in fact, which is surprisingly and delightfully urbane in this context.

40. *44–45 Baxtergate*

In the nineteenth century the first credits should go to the engineers. Whitby had had its two piers, carried on baulks of wood, since Tudor times. The East Pier had been rebuilt in stone about 1702. The West Pier was not reconstructed in stone until 1814. The two lighthouses (41) came somewhat later: on the

42. *Whitby Railway Station*

west side in 1831 and on the east in 1854. The West Pier Lighthouse is handsome. It consists of a fluted Doric column seventy feet high, crowned by an octagonal lantern.

The railway appeared in 1835, which was surprisingly early. The first six miles, from Whitby to Grosmont, were opened in that year; the other eighteen, across the moors to Pickering, a year later. (This latter is the very same line which, after closure in 1965, was reopened in 1973 under private ownership as the North Yorkshire Moors Railway.) But the odd thing about the original line, which was built to carry ironstone from Grosmont, timber from the nearby forests and farm produce from the Vale of Pickering, all to Whitby Harbour, was that originally only horses provided the traction; it was indeed expressly laid down in the original Act that steam locomotives must not be used. All this changed in 1847, when steam was introduced; that was the year which saw the opening of the Station (42), a pleasing building in sandstone which was probably designed by the excellent Yorkshire architect George Andrews, and which is still in use.

With the advent of steam, traffic greatly increased. George Hudson, known as 'the Railway King', was at this moment at the height of his success. He saw his chance, bought an extensive area of land on the West Cliff, and started to develop it for visitors. The Royal Hotel, the long white building in the most prominent position (43), was opened in 1848, and is still in business. But not many years later Hudson, who was a crooked financier, went bankrupt. Not until the 1870s did another entrepreneur, Sir George Elliott, take up the work that Hudson had relinquished. A Crescent was started, but not completed; it would never have been of any consequence architecturally. The enterprise culminated in the Metropole Hotel of 1897–8, a poor thing indeed compared with the Grand at Scarborough. This building is now flats.

Meanwhile, a second railway line, from Middlesbrough to Redcar and thence along the coast, had reached Whitby in 1883; it was continued to Scarborough two years later. This 'high-level' line is the one that crossed the 'great viaduct' referred to by Bram Stoker in my opening quotation. Larpool viaduct, a most graceful red-brick structure about a mile south-west of the town, is still there, and can be crossed on foot; but the railway, alas, is no more.

Whitby has a good deal of Victorian housing on the West Cliff, and very uninspiring it is. Victorian houses are not often listed by the Department of the Environment, and usually in my opinion rightly not. But Wellclose Square has at No. 9 (44) a villa which might well qualify. The banded rustication below, the Ionic pilasters of the doorcase, the boldly eared architraves to the upstairs windows, and not least the present-day grey livery over cement rendering, with details picked out in white: all these contribute, in my view, to the creation of a small house of real distinction.

Another Victorian building, the Seamen's Hospital (45), benefited some years ago from a repairs grant made by the Historic Buildings Council and the local authorities under the Town Scheme established for Whitby in 1975. The front of this Victorian Jacobean almshouse, with a touch of Baroque at the centre,

43. Whitby from St Mary's churchyard

45 (right). *The Seamen's Hospital, Church Street*

44 (left). *9 Wellclose Square*

is in good red brick laid in English bond. It dates from 1842, and the great surprise is that it is an early work of George Gilbert Scott. But all the pleasure is in the façade; they travel economy class behind.

In our own day it would be too much to hope that bad architectural bloomers will not constantly be made. A small-scale example can be seen in Victoria Square (46). No. 6, on the left, is a neat little late-Georgian villa, in brick. If you should inherit such a house, and want to spoil it completely, a glance at the two adjoining houses will show you just how to do it.

But happily there is also much recent work that can be commended. Close to Flowergate was built, about 1980, a large new supermarket, by a firm which deserves to be named: County Properties of Scarborough. Within, it is exactly like any other supermarket; and so it should be. But externally the facing material is brick, and they troubled to provide a fascinating grouping of pantiled roofs (48), in the full spirit of Whitby. What a splendid thing to do. The result is that this big building, so far from being an eyesore as supermarkets so often are, is a considerable visual asset to the town, which is of great importance, as it is prominent in many views.

46 (right). *6–8 Victoria Square*

47 (left). *New housing by the harbour*

48 (below left). *Hintons Supermarket*

Recent housing here is also much above the average (47). If any concrete has been used, it is, quite rightly, not in evidence. The facing material is red brick of quite good quality. The roofs are pitched, as in England they always should be; in our climate the flat roof is a persistent anomaly. And, once again, they are all covered with pantiles. The colours are right; the scale is right; the materials are right.

A view looking south-west (49) reveals how harmoniously the new buildings integrate with the old. With a single exception (near the skyline) there is not a discordant note. There are no high-rise buildings anywhere; here, of all places, they would be an affront. There is a real feeling for the *genius loci*: the spirit of the place. And how often can that be said today? In a single phrase, Whitby has preserved its identity.

49. *Whitby looking south-west*

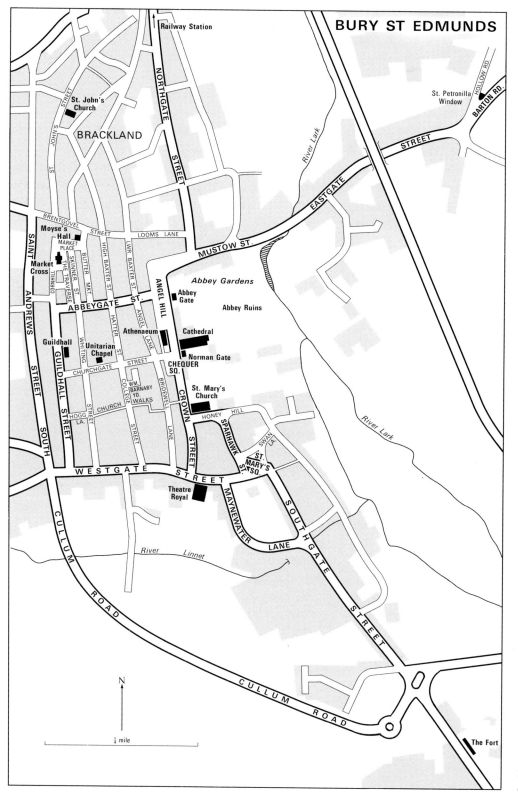

BURY ST EDMUNDS

Railway Station

St. Petronilla
Window

HOLLOW RD.

BARTON RD.

STREET

River Lark

EASTGATE

St. John's
Church

NORTHGATE STREET

BRACKLAND

SAINT JOHN'S ST.

BRENTGOVEL STREET

LOOMS LANE

MUSTOW ST.

Moyse's
Hall

MARKET
PLACE

Market
Cross

THE TRAVERSE

THINGOL

BUTTER ST.

SKINNER ST.

HIGH BAXTER ST.

LWR. BAXTER ST.

Abbey Gardens

Abbey
Gate

Abbey Ruins

ABBEYGATE ST.

ANGEL HILL

HATTER ST.

ANGEL LANE

Athenaeum

Cathedral

SAINT ANDREWS STREET

Guildhall

Unitarian
Chapel

WHITING ST.

GUILDHALL STREET

CHURCHGATE STREET

WM.
BARNABY
YD.

COLLEGE STREET

CHURCH STREET

HOGG LA.

BRIDEWELL LANE

Norman Gate

CHEQUER
SQ.

St. Mary's
Church

WALKS

CROWN STREET

Honey Hill

SPARHAWK ST.

SWAN LA.

River Lark

ST.
MARY'S
SQ.

SOUTH

WESTGATE STREET

Theatre
Royal

MAYNEWATER LANE

SOUTHGATE STREET

CULLUM ROAD

River Linnet

N

¼ mile

CULLUM ROAD

The Fort

1. *Plan of Bury*
St Edmunds

BURY ST EDMUNDS

I wonder how many people, outside Suffolk perhaps, could answer the quiz question: Which English town is situated on two rivers, the Lark and Linnet? They are small birds and, appropriately enough, small rivers: the Linnet minuscule. But the answer is not as easy as might be supposed, for some people would now say St Edmundsbury (written in one word) while others would reply Bury St Edmunds. The former now figures on the title-page of the town's Official Guide and is supported by town government as well, of course, as by the Diocese, but almost everyone else still calls the place Bury St Edmunds, which is usually abbreviated to Bury, *tout simple*.

How delightful, all the same, to be built upon the banks of the Linnet and the Lark. It puts one in a good temper straight away, just to think of that.

There was a small monastery here even in the seventh century. That was sacked by the Danes, but refounded by Canute in 1020 after his conversion to Christianity. It prospered exceedingly, especially under Baldwin, who was Abbot for over thirty years: from 1065 to 1097. In his time there were eighty Benedictine monks.

It was Baldwin who, about 1080, laid out the town on the grid plan which to this day survives (1). Bury and Ludlow were perhaps the two most deliberately planned towns in England during the Middle Ages. The town came into being, like Cirencester, to serve the Abbey, and the analogy with the Cotswold town persists. At Bury too, whereas the town is now very prosperous, the Abbey has suffered disastrously.

The Church was enormous: over 500 feet long. Except at the west end only some unlovely flint fragments remain. The west front, at 246 feet, was easily the widest in the country. Much of it was later converted into houses (2), which are now looking rather down at heel. Some archaeologically inclined people would like to see the later additions removed. In my view this would be a mistake. Flint ruins never make any appeal aesthetically. The right course, surely, would be to restore these houses so that they make a positive contribution to the scene. At present, it must be admitted, they are with one exception something of an eyesore.

As for the rest of the Abbey complex, here is what John Leland wrote about it in 1534: 'A man who saw the Abbey would say verily it were a city, so many gates there are in it, and some of brass: so many towers and a most stately church, upon which attend three other churches, also standing gloriously in the same churchyard, all of passing fine and curious workmanship.'

3 (right). *The Dovecot*

2 (left). *Houses in the Abbey west front*

A few relics of the Abbey's great days do still give pleasure. There is the hexagonal Dovecot (3), roofless but otherwise fairly well preserved; although mainly built of random flint, limestone was employed for the quoins and also for the Tudor windows on the upper storey. Nearby is the so-called Abbot's Bridge (4) across the Lark. The distinctive feature of this bridge is that it carries not only a footway but the lofty perimeter wall of the Abbey precinct. The outer face is the more attractive. Dating originally from about 1200, it was strengthened during the fourteenth century by the addition of a pair of massive flying buttresses and gabled piers. Each arch formerly embodied a portcullis, which could be lowered to water-level in order to prevent entry by boat.

But far and away the greatest survivors of the Abbey are the two gatehouses. The Norman Gate (5) was exactly in front of the West door of the Church, and it looks straight up Churchgate Street, one of the principal arteries of the town in Abbot Baldwin's plan. The builder, between 1120 and 1148, was Abbot Anselm. The material is Barnack oolitic limestone from near Stamford, whence it was brought in flat-bottomed boats across the Fens, not then drained, up the Ouse and into its tributary, the Lark: a long journey but perfectly feasible. The Barnack quarries belonged to the monks of Peterborough, from whom the Bury monks from time to time acquired quarrying rights. It is an excellent stone, but 850 years is a very long time, and considerable restoration took place in 1846. The original battlements had crumbled and were not put back. Instead, two lively and original gargoyles were added on the north and south faces. The angles of the tower are strong and plain; the intervening walls, designed

4 (right). *Abbot's Bridge*

5 (left). *The Norman Gate*

in four stages, are richly elaborated. Although at some little distance from the Cathedral, this noble tower, which has ten bells hung in 1785, now serves as its belfry. It is unfortunate that owing to the raising of the level of the road, as a precaution against flooding, its base is no longer easily seen.

By the fourteenth century, here as in many other English towns, the monks had become very unpopular, and in 1327, on the accession of Edward III, the people of Bury could stand no more. The Abbey was sacked and parts were burnt. Understandably, the monks took fright and proceeded greatly to strengthen their defences. The walls of the Precinct were heightened, and a new gate-

6 (right). *Abbey Gate*

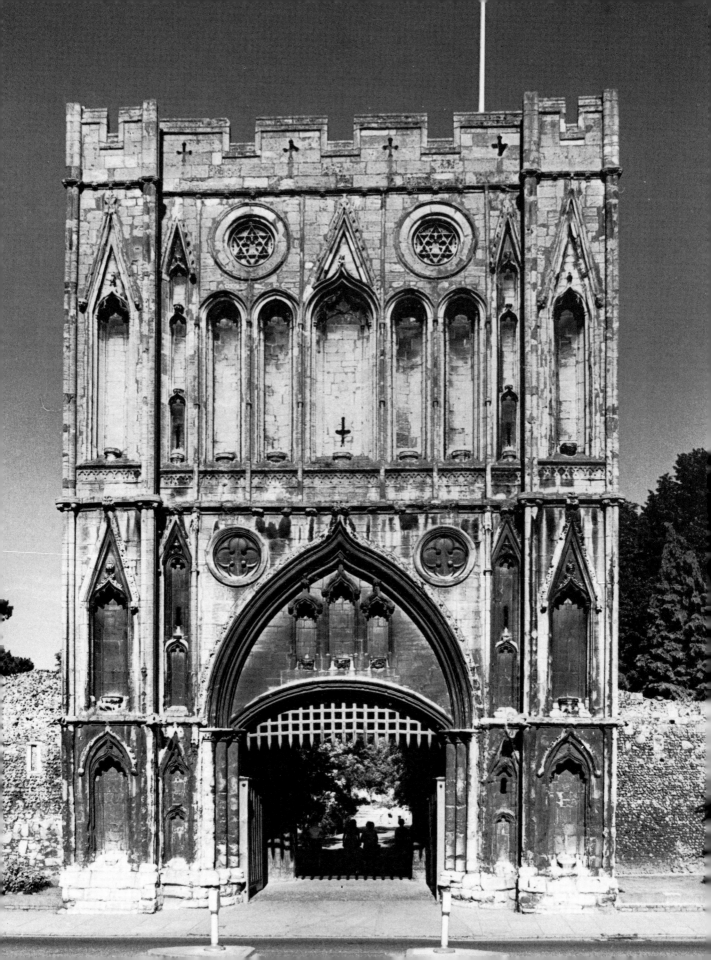

house was built to replace the one that had been destroyed. Abbey Gate (6), as it is called, was finished in 1353. It has lost the pair of octagonal turrets, each fourteen feet high, which originally surrounded the outer angles, nor is it as lofty as the Norman Gate. But it is much less restored, and still finer as a work of art. It is at once strong – notice the portcullis (a replacement) and the arrow slits – and exquisitely enriched: one of Bury's most treasured possessions.

It must be said that, unpopular though they often were and no doubt deserved to be, the monks did some good things too. One was the founding of hospitals. Bury had five. A mile to the north-east of the town centre can be seen a beautiful fifteenth-century window (7) which recalls one of them, the Hospital of St Petronilla, founded to care for lepers. This is not on its original site. The date of its removal does not seem to have been recorded, but the happy juxtaposition with the great cedar tree points surely to a piece of 'picturesque' garden layout during the Georgian period. It now adjoins the site of another hospital, St Nicholas, which has also all but disappeared.

Bury preserves only two medieval churches, and they are very nearly side by side. St Mary is in origin much the older; when the present church was built in the fifteenth century, it was the fifth one to occupy this site. Until a few

7 (far left).
Window from the
Hospital of
St Petronilla
8 (above).
St Mary's Church

years ago it was also slightly the larger of the two, and undoubtedly the finer. Although parts are faced with limestone, the basic material is, again, flint: Bury's only local building stone. The robust tower, not very lofty, is eccentrically sited close to the west end of the north aisle, providing an enjoyable and unexpected view when approached from the south (8).

The outstanding feature of the interior (9) is the beautiful roof of the nave.

9. *St Mary, the nave*

The structure consists of arched braces and hammer-beams in alternation; the latter take the form of big recumbent angels. And at the base of the long wall-posts, standing on embattled corbels, are no fewer than forty-two smaller figures: saints and more angels, martyrs, prophets and kings. The arcade, all stone-faced, is lofty and elegant. The bad feature here is the Victorian glass, which darkens the church without enriching it; the dirty-green glass in all the clerestory windows cries out for replacement by clear glass.

The other church, St James, was in 1913 elevated to cathedral rank, and since 1960 has been transformed. Originally erected by Abbot Anselm in the twelfth century, it was, like St Mary, wholly rebuilt later: in this case not until the Tudor period. The nave has high, elegant arcades and lofty aisles (11). The architect was almost certainly the great John Wastell, whose other achievements include the Bell Harry tower at Canterbury, the fan-vaulted retrochoir at Peterborough and, his masterpiece, King's College chapel at Cambridge. His home was at Bury, where he died in 1515. Except in one window, the glass is all Victorian, but of a very much better quality than next door. The old nave roof was nearly flat, but the present one is also Victorian: a somewhat timid hammer-beam roof designed by George Gilbert Scott. The elaborate colour scheme of 1982 replaces the one first introduced here in 1949.

10. *Cathedral, the new choir from the south*

11. *Cathedral, the nave*

But to operate effectively as a cathedral, St James needed considerable enlargement. Shortage of money and ever-rising costs following two world wars caused long delays, but at last, in 1959, an architect was appointed: Stephen Dykes Bower. The project is not yet complete; in particular, it is hoped one day to have a lofty central tower and spire. But the new choir (10) is finished, and, though quite different in elevation from the nave and considerably loftier, the exterior is enriched with flushwork (the use of flint in conjunction with dressed stone to form decorative panels, etc.) in the best East Anglian tradition. The dark knapped flints are an excellent foil to the light-toned limestone (12). Most of this came from Doulting in Somerset, the same as was employed for the Cathedral of Wells. But for the string courses, copings and mouldings Clipsham stone from Rutland was used.

Few problems are more difficult for an architect than to extend harmoniously an old church. Many fail through excessive concern with their own individuality: they must, they feel, 'be themselves' and add 'something different'. This is a mistake. The new architect need not, indeed should not, be a mere copyist, but he should respect the architecture of the building with which he is concerned. His additions can be self-confident, but they must not be discordant.

12 (far left). *Cathedral, south side of choir*
13 (above). *Cathedral, choir ceiling*

In my view, this is exactly what Dykes Bower has achieved at Bury. He has had plenty of his own to offer, but all that he has done is harmonious. Happily, no attempt has been made to be self-consciously modern.

The new choir is lofty and light, and colour has been used with considerable resource. The three East windows are mainly filled with acceptable Victorian glass by Kempe from the side windows of the former chancel. The panelled and painted roofs (13) have a tapestry quality. The iron screens, painted red and blue, silver and gold, are completely original. The panels, believe it or not, were grilles for underfloor heating which the architect had the imagination to retrieve from a Victorian church near Manchester. Their re-use here is most successful. At the crossing the structure is of reinforced concrete – just as it would have been in the Middle Ages, had the architects of those days known of this material – but the facing of the four soaring arches (11) is Doulting freestone. The outcome is an interior which is at once spacious and dignified, and, surely, an outstandingly good example of the way to convert a parish church into a cathedral.

14, 15. *Moyse's Hall*

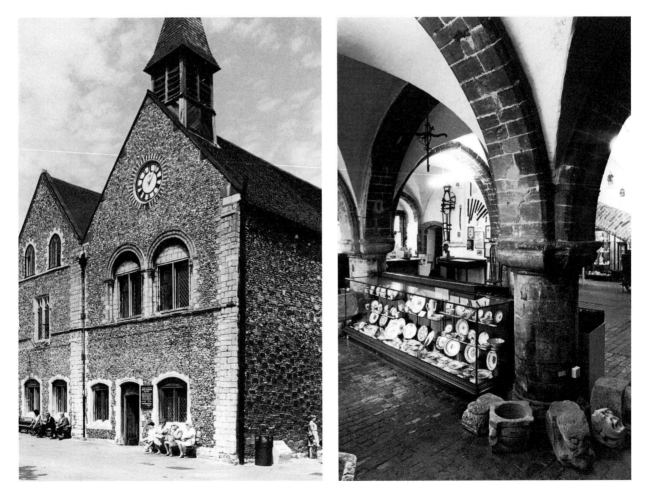

It is time to turn to Bury's secular buildings, which of course are far more numerous.

On the domestic side there is one of England's very few surviving Norman houses. Moyse's Hall (14), built needless to say wholly of stone, dates from about 1180. Most of the stone, inevitably, is flint. Externally, it cannot be said that this building any longer carries much conviction. All the windows have been changed; the side wall and the roof have been renewed; there is an inappropriate clock and that ridiculous turret. The only ostensibly Norman feature is the pair of moulded arches framing the windows above the entrance.

The interior (15) is much better preserved. The great surprise is to find that the ground-floor rooms have groined vaults springing from cushion capitals which are borne on sturdy circular piers. Why, we ask, were there not just wooden ceilings? Why such a show of strength? The likely explanation is that the Jewish builder was a moneylender, so needed what was in a sense his own private strongroom. Its later history was chequered. For nearly three hundred years, until 1610, it was an inn. In the eighteenth century it became a workhouse, and then a gaol. After that it served for a while as a railway parcels office. Finally, in 1899, it became what it still is: the Borough museum, serving to illustrate the life of the town and surrounding district through the centuries.

But much more enjoyable architecturally is the former Guildhall (16). This delightful building dates from the latter part of the fifteenth century, although inside the porch there is a stone doorway, reset, which is over two hundred years older. The wings, in so-called white brick, were refronted in 1807. For hundreds of years this was the meeting place of the town council, which only moved in 1966 to the Shire Hall. The special feature is the porch, which effectively epitomises the variety of building materials to be found in Bury. The side walls are mostly flint, coursed but in crude lumps. On the front, however, the flints are knapped and laced with bands of thin red brick, and above, on the deep parapet, combined with squares of limestone to make an effective chequer pattern. The lowest stage of this front is entirely faced with ashlared limestone, as are the octagonal corner turrets. Of limestone also are the string courses and the battlements, with pretty quatrefoils in the merlons. Towards the end of the eighteenth century the pair of windows were renewed, while below them was added the charming carved escutcheon with the coat of arms of the Borough. It would be good if the assertive notice-board could be repositioned.

For hundreds of years, however, Bury was essentially a timber-framed town. Nor did it escape one of those devastating fires to which wooden housing – not, of course, excepting London itself, in 1666 – was so often exposed. Bury's great fire came in 1608. But what is interesting is that for the rebuilding the principal material here was still wood.

16. *The Old Guildhall*

Even Cupola House (18), the one house that Celia Fiennes admired when she visited the town in 1698, is timber-framed, as the jetty above the ground-floor rooms reveals. This large, attractive house – which is now a restaurant, therefore accessible – had been built just five years before, for an affluent apothecary. The attractive topknot, a fashionable feature at that time, to which the building owes its name, is unfortunately not seen in the photograph.

Otherwise, Miss Fiennes was not impressed with Bury's houses. Though 'there are a great deal of Gentry here', she recorded, 'there are no good houses, but only what are old and rambling.' What the visitor will quickly realise is that almost all the old timber-framed houses that have survived have been very much restored and altered. Celia Fiennes refers, perhaps a trifle condescendingly, to 'houses of timber mostly in the old form' with 'long peaked roofes of tileing'. Nos. 16–18 Bridewell Lane (17) was no doubt one of them: one moreover that escaped the fire. This was an early Tudor hall-house: that is to say, with a hall in the centre which went right up to the roof. But presently

17 (far left). *16–18 Bridewell Lane*
18 (above). *Cupola House, The Traverse*

19 (top right). *Martin's, Cornhill*
20 (right). *61–63 Whiting Street*

21. *20 Hatter Street*

the hall was divided horizontally by the insertion of a floor, and then the house was divided vertically and sash-framed windows were inserted. In about the 1830s No. 16 was given a handsome Doric doorcase with fluted columns and a triglyph frieze. Whether this suits the house is another matter!

It will be observed that there are now no exposed timbers, as on this house there would have been originally. But any framed house post-dating the fire of 1608 is likely to have been rendered from the outset, since East Anglia has never been as enthusiastic about exposed timbers as, say, the Welsh border counties. The most spectacular example of exposed timbering is, amusingly enough, the superstructure of a shop erected at the end of the nineteenth century by Boots the chemists (19). Above the truly dreadful fascia board of the present occupants, the building bursts forth into a glorious riot of mock timber-framing and stucco ornamentation such as only the Jacobeans or the Victorians would have dared to perpetrate. It is very enjoyable, but was only just saved from destruction a few years ago by the activity of local preservationists.

Elsewhere, it will be found that gabled houses have nearly all been rendered. When timbers are exposed, as at 61–63 Whiting Street (20), there has generally been drastic restoration. Like 16–18 Bridewell Lane, this too started life as a single hall-house. No. 61 (on the left) has, under the overhang, what was once an early nineteenth-century shop-window. Another was inserted at No. 20 Hatter Street (21), a seventeenth-century timber-framed and plastered house which is instructive for anyone interested in windows. Each time the eye moves upwards, it retreats a century. The shop-window is in the early nineteenth-

22. 11 Abbeygate Street

century style. The first-floor windows are Georgian, double-hung sashes with all their glazing bars. And on the second floor, in the gables, are casement windows with leaded lights, which no doubt the whole house had when it was first erected.

Old shop-windows are not a rarity in Bury. Indeed, I cannot recall any other English town which has managed to keep so many shop-fronts that are a real pleasure to look at. The buildings themselves may well be timber-framed structures dating from the seventeenth century, even though the upstairs windows will usually have been altered. No. 11 Abbeygate Street (22) is a Grade I building with an exceptionally fine six-window shop-front in the Gothick manner, dating from soon after 1800. No. 4 Angel Hill (23) was much altered in the Georgian period and its principal shop-front is of that date. Nos. 66–67 Guildhall Street (24) was a good deal spoiled, I would think early in the present century, but two of the three late-Georgian shop-windows survive intact. Nos. 35–36 Abbeygate Street (25) is structurally a red-brick building of Queen Anne's time with a robust modillioned eaves-cornice; the shop-fronts, one bowed, belong to the early nineteenth century. Nos. 31–33 Angel Hill (26)

is a Regency terrace in grey brick with all its upper windows intact, and here the shops (now a restaurant) may well be contemporary with the rest.

But if the interior is also taken into account, the best of all Bury's shops is also the oldest: 56 Abbeygate Street (27). Early in the nineteenth century this timber-framed building was refronted in stucco, but the structure is over two hundred years older. In fact the oak corner-post, which is fortunately protected by the present window, has carved figures (30) which are believed to go back to the early years of Henry VIII. Inside are framed oak roofs, here and there enriched with brattishing (31), a moulding derived from small conventionalised leaves, which is quite common on Gothic church screens. There is also a Jacobean staircase with lovely newel posts, and upstairs a striking tie-beam roof with crown-posts (29). A framed building such as this one was prefabricated. Each joint was carefully marked in the carpenters' yard, so that the builders could fit the correct mortices over the right tenons. Some of these axe marks can still be seen here. This shop, which also has, on the side elevation, a Doric porch (28), has been connected with pharmacy and medicine for not far short of three hundred years. Admirably maintained, it must be one of the most beautiful in England.

30 (left),
31 (below).
56 Abbeygate Street, corner-post and ceiling

The great event of the eighteenth century, architecturally speaking, was, here as in many other English country towns, the advent of brick. Before 1700 its use in Bury had been very sparing indeed. It now became so popular that within a few years no substantial builder thought of using anything else.

32. *Unitarian Chapel, Churchgate Street*

The first memorable building in this material is a most surprising one: the Presbyterian Chapel, now Unitarian, built in 1711–12 (32). This is a nonconformist chapel of quite unusual distinction – and Suffolk has another very good one at Ipswich, but that is timber-framed. There are patches of modern repointing which make one weep, but the brickwork, laid still in English bond (that is, with alternating courses of headers and stretchers), is of very fine quality in two shades of red, with rubbed brick employed for the dressings. Specially attractive are the oval window in the centre and the lifting of the attic cornice in an arc over the sundial. Originally there would almost certainly have been stone urns or vases on the parapet, and it is a pity that these have been lost. But valiant efforts have been made in recent years to restore a building which used to look sadly decrepit.

Nearly twenty years later (1730) came the Clopton Asylum (33), situated in the grounds of the Abbey, and abutting on to the site of the church itself. With its stately seven-bay centre flanked by projecting wings, and a splendid coat of arms in the pediment, this might well be taken for the former town house of some grandee; but not at all! It was erected as an almshouse, and most of it is now the residence of the Provost of the Cathedral, and known as Provost's House.[1]

Elsewhere, however, the leading West Suffolk families were building big town houses in Bury. None is by a known professional architect, and none perhaps is outstanding, but cumulatively they do give a vivid impression of what a thriving place this was during the Georgian period. Not that there was much industry. There was prosperous farming round about, and Bury was the market town for the produce of the farms. There was also the Fair, a famous event which for centuries was held annually on Angel Hill during the second half of September. People came to Bury Fair from far and near and even from abroad, especially from Holland. There was trading, of course, but there was much entertainment too: it was a great social occasion.

[1] A matter which frequently puzzles the layman is why some modern cathedrals have a dean, others a provost. The nomenclature depends upon whether or not there are also parochial responsibilities. At Bury there are, so he is the Provost. At Guildford, for example, there are not, so he is the Dean.

33. *Provost's House, formerly the Clopton Asylum*

The most imposing of these town houses, all in red brick, was erected by the Herveys of Ickworth. (John Hervey was created Earl of Bristol in 1715, but the huge oval house at Ickworth, now the property of the National Trust, was not built until much later.) Their mansion at Bury was known as The Manor House (34). It was designed in 1736 for the then Countess of Bristol by Sir James Burrough, a Cambridge don and amateur architect who later became Master of Gonville and Caius College. Although very well built and on a lordly scale, it is externally no masterpiece – although it would have greatly benefited from the big coat of arms which must surely at one time have adorned the pediment. The interior is better, with a good staircase and fine ceilings, doorcases and chimney-pieces. It would make a splendid art gallery, but unfortunately there is no early likelihood of its being used for that purpose. It accommodates a department of the County Council, and although well maintained is much too good to be used as offices.

More interesting architecturally, and only a little less grand, is No. 8 Northgate Street (35). This was a Georgian rebuilding of an earlier house, and at the rear some timber-framing still survives. The recessed centre is most unexpected. There is a deep porch with an elaborate frieze supported by clustered

34. *The Manor House, 5 Honey Hill*

pilasters, a very handsome Venetian window framed in stone, and another size-able round-headed window above. The builder of this house is not known; but the long low building next door, now divided, was once the town house of the Gages from Hengrave Hall, one of whom introduced the greengage into England.

Southgate House (36), built about 1728, is notable for its excellent brickwork. Unexpectedly, it has a half-hipped mansard roof. This house, with handsome wrought-iron gates, stands in its own grounds nearly a mile south-east of the town centre. No. 82 Guildhall Street (37) is an agreeable George II house which in due course was bought by James Oakes, a local banker. In 1789 he asked Soane to enlarge it, and it was he who added the two pedimented wings with tripartite ground-floor windows under recessed elliptical arches. He executed the commission with exquisite tact and in a wholly unselfassertive spirit: the only regret is that this long elevation abuts on to a thoroughfare so narrow and so busy.

Before the end of the eighteenth century red bricks went out of fashion. If you could build in what was euphemistically called white brick, which was really dun-coloured or a pale, dusty-looking yellow-grey, you generally did so. This was closer in colour to stone, which was the ideal, but at Bury usually too expensive.

In order to make 'white' bricks it was necessary to find clay with a good

35. *8 Northgate Street*

deal of lime in its composition, and no or very little iron, for it is that which causes most bricks to emerge from their kilns some shade of red. Not every part of England has the right clays for this, but at Bury there was no problem. The Gault clays of Cambridgeshire yielded large quantities of these bricks, but Bury builders did not even have to rely only on these, for in the Suffolk chalk, around Woolpit, a few miles to the east, there were Pleistocene clays which were equally suitable.

Nos. 5 and 6 St Mary's Square (38), the home of Thomas Clarkson, MP, who promoted the Slavery Emancipation Bill in 1833, was originally one house, built in the closing years of the eighteenth century. Here the two colours are both in evidence: the basic one is 'white', but red was still being employed for all the dressings. But a few years later, at 4 Chequer Square (39), red had disappeared altogether. The moulded bands at two levels, which add variety and distinction to this imposing front, are of stucco.

Nos. 1 and 2 Angel Hill (41) would appear to have been built about 1830. Here again there is not a red brick to be seen. Although at both these houses, for some odd reason, the glazing bars were later removed from the ground-floor windows, these two are not a pair. There are many differences. At No. 1 the shallow porch is Doric, and centrally placed. At No. 2 it is Ionic, and not central, though both elevations are five windows wide. At No. 2 the first-floor windows are carried down to the floor, and a delicate balcony was added, no doubt as part of the original design, for Regency clients loved balconies and long windows. Under this balcony is a small plaque: one of a number in Bury, all tantalisingly uninformative! LOUIS PHILIPPE KING OF FRANCE b.1773

40. *Priory Hotel, Mildenhall Road, south side*

d.1850. Yes, but what did he *do* here? Have a cup of coffee? We are not told.

These two houses also effectively illustrate the pros and cons of creepers. But the partial mantling of No. 2 pales into insignificance beside the display, exuberant or horrific according to taste, on No. 3, the Angel Hotel (43). This is also built of 'white' brick, but we are hardly aware of it. Such is the fame of the Angel, so prestigious is its history (it figures, of course, in *Pickwick Papers*), that to cavil at its festoons of creeper would be regarded in some eyes as *lèse-majesté*. Personally I deplore them; the Angel has been described as like a big shaggy dog, and shaggy coats require vigorous combing. What is, however, certain is that this superabundant display is not in any way a product of neglect; it is deliberate, and, for better or worse, it has become part of the personality of the building.

41. *1–2 Angel Hill*

Despite the triumph of brick here from the time of Queen Anne onwards, Bury never lost its liking also for stucco. There was, moreover, a generally approved colour, to which nearly everyone conformed: peach-pink. So popular was this colour in this part of England that it became known as 'Suffolk pink'. Unfortunately, the traditional colour has become difficult to procure; the colour that is in general use now is known as dusky pink. Plenty of that can now be seen in and around Bury. The shade varies a little; the further away it gets from strawberry ice cream the better. If I were covering a stucco surface with this colour, I would always mix in a small quantity of yellow before applying it. Thereby one could return to the real, authentic Suffolk pink.

42 (right). *3 Looms Lane*
43 (far right). *The Angel Hotel, 3 Angel Hill*

A large house built under Elizabeth I on the site of the Franciscan Friary a mile to the north of the Abbey is now the Priory Hotel. Most of it is timber-framed and many-gabled, with some fine brick chimney-stacks, but on the south side, in the Georgian period, it was refronted in brick and rendered (40). The

colour is Suffolk pink. So is that of The Acacias in Looms Lane (42), which is now a restaurant. This engaging Regency villa, with a characteristic verandah, was built of a mixture of flint and white brick, as a glance at the side wall will confirm, but good architectural manners evidently dictated that the front should be both rendered and coloured.

44 (left). *The Athenaeum*

45 (right). *Athenaeum ballroom*

These handsome houses tell their own story. Bury, during the eighteenth century, had become a highly flourishing social centre. Even in 1723 Daniel Defoe had described it as being 'the town of all this part of England, in proportion to its bigness, [that is] most thronged with gentry, people of the best fashion, and the most polite conversation'. 'This beauty and healthiness of situation', he went on perceptively, 'was no doubt the occasion which drew the clergy to settle here, for they always choose the best places in the country to build in, either for richness of soil or for health and pleasure in the situation of their religious houses.' Such people always wanted assembly rooms, coffee rooms, a ballroom, a theatre. After all, they had to do *something*!

Assembly rooms were probably first opened here in, or soon after, 1713. The building, now called the Athenaeum (44), was re-edified in 1789, when the original top storey was removed, and altered again fifteen years later, probably by the architect Francis Sandys, who was living at the time next door, at No. 1 Angel Hill (cf p. 103). The exterior, of rendered brick with a portico, is not Suffolk pink; here the colour, whatever it was originally, is now *eau-de-nil*, and very pleasant it is. The dome, also green, is a nineteenth-century addition and is not the feature which it might have been. A good dome would have

46 (right). *Theatre Royal*

47. *Market Cross*

been architecturally a great improvement to this building, which is very promi-
nently sited at the south end of Angel Hill. But the interior contains a delightful
ballroom in the Adam style (45), with delicate stucco decoration on the vault
and, half-way along one side, a columned recess for the band. The special feature is the double staircase, most elegantly contrived.

Then, after the Napoleonic war, came the Theatre Royal, designed by William Wilkins, the architect of the National Gallery. The exterior is unmemor-
able, but within is one of the most agreeable early theatres in the country (46).
After falling into disuse and being appropriated by the neighbouring brewery
for the storage of beer barrels, it had a miraculous resurrection. In 1965 it

was reopened as a theatre, and comfortably reseated. This is a rare example of a late-Georgian playhouse with pit, boxes and gallery, entirely delightful unless you are unlucky enough to get a seat behind one of the iron columns! It now belongs to the National Trust, for whom some years ago I had the pleasure of lecturing here; and, although there was no microphone, the acoustics are so good that I was told that all the 350 people who filled the theatre heard perfectly.

This was not, however, Bury's first theatre, which was in what Nikolaus Pevsner termed the town's finest post-medieval building, and no wonder, for the architect who reconstructed it between 1774 and 1780 was none other than Robert Adam (47). This had been the Market Hall: Adam, in his reconstruction, provided for a small theatre upstairs. The ground floor, which was originally open, continued to be used for markets; after the opening of the Theatre Royal in 1819, the upper part became the Town Hall (although, as already mentioned, the town council continued to meet at the Guildhall). This lofty room now serves as a gallery for exhibitions. The building has been renamed the Market Cross, for no better reason than that it occupies the site of the medieval cross. This is surely very confusing; a cross is not a substantial building, as this is.

Adam certainly gave Bury one of its most enjoyable possessions. It occupies an island site, and if not a cross it is at least cruciform. Although the basic material is grey brick, the lower storey is entirely faced with rusticated limestone, and the upper parts are also generously enriched. The design is full of subtleties. At the centre of each of the four fronts is a large Venetian window set within an Ionic aedicule. (Incidentally, the glazing of the arched window-heads varies: all those on the east (right) side are as they should be, but on the south (left) the bar runs up into the centre of the arch, which is not good.) Below all the principal windows are delicate stone balustrades, purely decorative in intention. Above are stone panels with swags and paterae. The ornaments of Etruscan type in the niches are of cast iron. The building (like so many others) would benefit from the removal of the ugly chimney-pots, which now probably serve no purpose.

So at last we are back with limestone, which because it had to be brought from a considerable distance was always something of a luxury at Bury. Yet the town's most spectacular stone-faced building was anything but luxurious! The old Gaol, now known as The Fort (48), dates from 1803. The architect, George Byfield, was no doubt inspired by George Dance the younger's Newgate Gaol in London, demolished in 1902. Of this building, too, only the façade now survives, but, with the exception of a single house (6 Honey Hill), this is the only secular building in the town to have been entirely faced with dressed stone.

This is Ketton stone from Rutland, said to be structurally the most perfect of all the oolitic limestones, because of its freedom from interspersed shell fragments. The quality of the masonry is superb. The centre (49) is both rusticated and vermiculated. Rustication involves recessed joints, and therefore shadows, which induce a feeling of additional strength, very appropriate to a gaol. Vermiculation (50) is the term used when, for purely ornamental reasons, the surface of a block of stone is dressed so that it appears to be covered with worm-tracks. It was an odd idea, but it can be, as here, surprisingly effective. This is formidable architecture. It must have had a severely deterrent effect upon intending criminals.

The principal contribution of the Victorian period was the development of Brackland, centred on the new church of St John, completed in 1841. This was a tall Woolpit-brick spire, which looks fine from a distance but not close to. Around it are a number of quiet streets of modest houses with mostly 'white' brick fronts and red backs and sides, revealing which was the more highly esteemed. Although without architectural pretensions, Brackland is a 'homely' area, with small 'villagey' shops which should surely be preserved: yet not so long ago it was under serious threat of demolition. It was this that prompted the formation of the now vigilant Bury Society.

At the northern end of this quarter is the Station, which should certainly not be forgotten, although it has already suffered a good deal. Erected in 1847, in the brightest red brick, it is quite unlike any other. The railway here is on a lofty embankment, and the building rises still higher, crowned as it is, on both sides of the tracks, by fancifully designed towers. There are also gables in the Dutch style and bold brackets in cast iron to support the roofs. The architect was Sancton Wood.

With the arrival of the railway Bury expanded, and in recent years this has been fast gathering momentum. It has become, inevitably, much more of a working town than it used to be. In the surrounding countryside farming is still the principal occupation, and in the town itself this activity is symbolised by the Corn Exchange (51), which is mainly grey brick but has a very imposing Ionic portico in, I think, Bath stone. The date is 1861–2, which was a time when people were somewhat prone to inscribe pious quotations on friezes and elsewhere. Hence, here (but not visible in this photograph because of the deep shadow) THE EARTH IS THE LORD'S AND THE FULLNESS THEREOF. Although in 1970 the sides were redesigned to accommodate shops, this building is still what it has always been: the Corn Exchange.

But the three chief places of employment are now in the brewery, in the sugar-beet factory, and in county and local government. Unfortunately all three have gone too high for comfort architecturally. The Victorian brewery dominates the west side of what would otherwise have been the town's most attractive

48. *The Fort*

49 (right). *Centrepiece*
50 (far right). *Rustication and vermiculation*

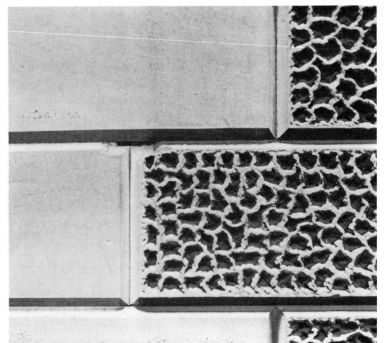

51. *Corn Exchange*

Square: St Mary's. The sugar-beet factory dates only from 1924, when there was a serious agricultural depression. This is well away from the historic town, so does no serious harm visually. Not so, alas, the addition to the Borough Council Offices made in the late sixties in Lower Baxter Street. This is a wretched building, from whatever angle it is seen.

As for traffic, it would be far from true to say that all the problems have yet been solved. But important steps have been taken, and in particular the diversion of the A45 road on to a new by-pass in 1973. This road aroused deep indignation in some quarters when it was first constructed, but in fact it has settled in tolerably well, and has certainly performed a great service in relieving Bury of much of its through traffic.

In the historic centre a complicated system of one-way streets renders it virtually impossible for a motorist to drive through it, and this is as it should be. The grid plan might be thought to simplify matters, but this is hardly the case because most of the streets in the old town are so narrow. The Market Place is spacious, but so it needs to be, for there is still a flourishing market here every Wednesday and Saturday.

Angel Hill is also a broad open space. Near the centre is a specially unenjoyable signpost known locally as the pillar of salt, but the slender modern lamp-posts (23, 26, 44) are almost elegant. This is largely because, thank goodness, they are of steel and not of concrete. On this subject I shall have more to say when we reach Devizes. Angel Hill's misfortune is that much of it is now a car park. An alternative site could only be provided by the demolition of outworn properties – and there are some – a little farther away. This, no doubt, would not please the car-owners, but it would greatly improve the town's showpiece.

Today, with a population of over 30,000 and still rising, Bury is growing larger than many people would wish to see it. But there has been a modest Town Scheme in operation since 1979, and both the Bury St Edmunds Society and the Suffolk Preservation Society have been very active here. A day would hardly suffice to relish all the good things which this town still has to offer. But the historic centre must be explored on foot; there is no other way.

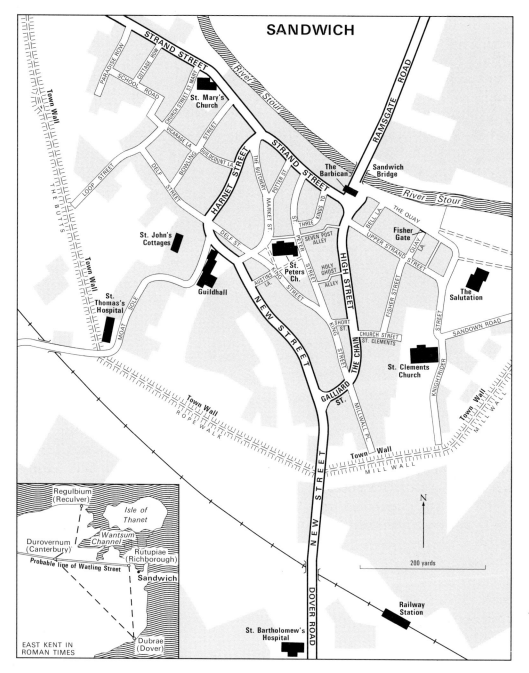

SANDWICH

Strand Street · Paradise Row · Cottage Row · School Road · Church Street · St Mary · Vicarage La. · Bowling Street · Guildcount La. · Loop Street · Delf Street · Harnet Street · The Butchery · Market St. · Potter St. · Strand Street · River Stour · The Barbican · Sandwich Bridge · River Stour · The Quay · Bella · Fisher Gate · Quay La. · Upper Strand Street

St. Mary's Church · St. John's Cottages · St. Peters Ch. · Three Kings Yd · Seven Post Alley · Holy Ghost Alley · Peter St · King St. · Austins La. · King Street · Short St · High Street · Fisher Street · The Salutation · Sandown Road · Church Street · St. Clements · St. Clements Church · Knightrider Street

Guildhall · St. Thomas's Hospital · Moat Sole · New Street · The Chain · Galliard St. · Millwall Pl. · Town Wall · Town Wall · Mill Wall · Ropewalk · Town Wall · Mill Wall

Town Wall · The Butts

N

200 yards

EAST KENT IN ROMAN TIMES

Regulbium (Reculver) · Isle of Thanet · Wantsum Channel · Durovernum (Canterbury) · Rutupiae (Richborough) · Probable line of Watling Street · Sandwich · Dubrae (Dover)

New Street · Dover Road · St. Bartholomew's Hospital · Railway Station

1. *Plan of Sandwich*

2 (inset). *East Kent in Roman times*

SANDWICH

Two thousand years ago, when the Romans first showed an interest in Britain, Thanet was still an island (2). As a place for a landing the Wantsum Channel, separating Thanet from the mainland, seemed ideal, for it was sheltered by sandbanks from the open sea. And so was founded Rutupiae, which we know as Richborough. From the year 43 until the end of the Roman occupation in 410, this was the principal port of communication between Britain and Gaul.

The settlement was on a low bluff above the sea, part of which disappeared when presently the sea encroached. Later the Wantsum Channel became silted up and the sea gradually receded. It is now a couple of miles away. But what have survived are long stretches of the walls of Richborough Castle, which enclose an area of more than five acres. They are still very imposing (3), and date from about 285, when the Romans became justifiably apprehensive about Saxon invasions. They were fully twenty-five feet high, and in some places, even now, they are not far short of that. The core is flint, with plenty of tough mortar. But the outer facing was stone masonry, with double courses of tiles at intervals. And outside the walls, for defensive purposes, ran two deep ditches: the mowing of their steep sides now presents quite a problem.

Sandwich, which is a mile or so to the south-east, did not appear on the scene until 664. The name was originally Sandwic, which meant a village or settlement upon a sandbank. That was still the spelling in the time of Henry VIII, as can be seen from Leland's *Itinerary*.

The land between Richborough and Sandwich is flat and uneventful. The only feature to catch the eye is the White Windmill (4), the sole survivor, it may be supposed, of an erstwhile colony of them. It is a smock mill, mostly weather-boarded, with a beehive cap, a fantail, and four sails nicely restored.

But Sandwich inherited from Richborough one valuable asset: the Roman road. Watling Street, which linked the coast with London and thence stalked across England – as, in the guise of the A5, it still does – to Verulamium (St Albans), Uriconium (Wroxeter) and thence to Deva (Chester), became throughout the Middle Ages a great artery of trade, especially for our wool and woven cloth. Sandwich was at the receiving end. It became the obvious port of embarkation, especially for the great market at Calais, which still belonged to us until 1558.

Like Richborough, Sandwich first gained significance as a port; it was, indeed, along with Dover, Hythe, Romney and Hastings, one of the original Cinque Ports. Rye and Winchelsea were soon added: and later seven others,

the 'limbs' as they were called, not all on the coast. (They were Lydd, Folke-stone, Deal, Ramsgate, Margate, Faversham and Tenterden.) The original confederation came into being before the Conquest, and from the time of Edward the Confessor was saddled with the responsibility of providing ships from their fishing fleets whenever the King wished to go abroad. This obligation was recorded in Domesday Book in 1086, and extended to other important people and even, on occasion, to the transport of whole armies. Moreover, the service had to be performed at the ports' own expense. But various privileges were granted in return, of which the most important was complete exemption from national taxation. Royal Charters also granted them trading concessions, freedom from tolls and customs duties, and the right to hold their own courts of law. To co-ordinate these matters the Crown appointed its own special representative: the Warden of the Cinque Ports. This ancient office still survives, as do some of the old customs and traditions, but the ship service had ceased even by the fifteenth century. By then the Navy had come into being, and the Navy, needless to say, demanded its own, much larger ships.

One obligation the inhabitants of Sandwich could not escape. Their feudal lord was the great Benedictine Abbey of Christ Church, Canterbury, and, in addition to having to pay an annual rent of £40, they were required to supply 40,000 (!) herrings a year for the degustation of the monks. But it would seem that they took this in their stride.

The growing prosperity of the Saxon-cum-Norman town suffered a sudden check in 1217, when it was devastated by French marauders. However, recovery

3. The ruins of Richborough Castle

4 (above). *The White Windmill*
5 (far right). *Sandwich, the ramparts*

would appear to have been rapid, and from the latter part of the thirteenth century Sandwich was for over a hundred years second only in importance to London as an English port. Yet it was not until the time of Richard II, when the place had over 3000 people and 800 houses, that it was for the first time, in the 1380s, provided with ramparts. And even then it was only facing the river, the Stour, that the walls were built of stone. Otherwise there were just a high bank of earth and a mostly dry moat. Today the walk along the ramparts (5) is one of the town's special pleasures, and on the landward side the circuit is complete.

By 1400 the shape and layout of this town were very much as they are today (1). There were five principal gates, of which only one, the Fisher Gate (6), now survives. The fourteenth-century part is of flint and stone, in a disorderly patchwork; the upper part, said to date from 1571 but looking decidedly Victorian, is in pale Gault brick.

Just outside the Fisher Gate the sluggish Stour meanders by. It used to be wider than it is now, and downstream there was plenty of anchorage in what was known as Sandwich Haven. Although such a flourishing port, Sandwich had never been quite on the coast; the safety of its haven was one of the attractions. But during the fifteenth century this advantage was gradually lost, for the river began to silt up, and just when ships were getting bigger.

Then in 1457, as a reprisal, it must be said, for raids on French ports, the adversary struck again. Sandwich suffered another devastating French attack. Although the town centre survived, everywhere else there was great destruction.

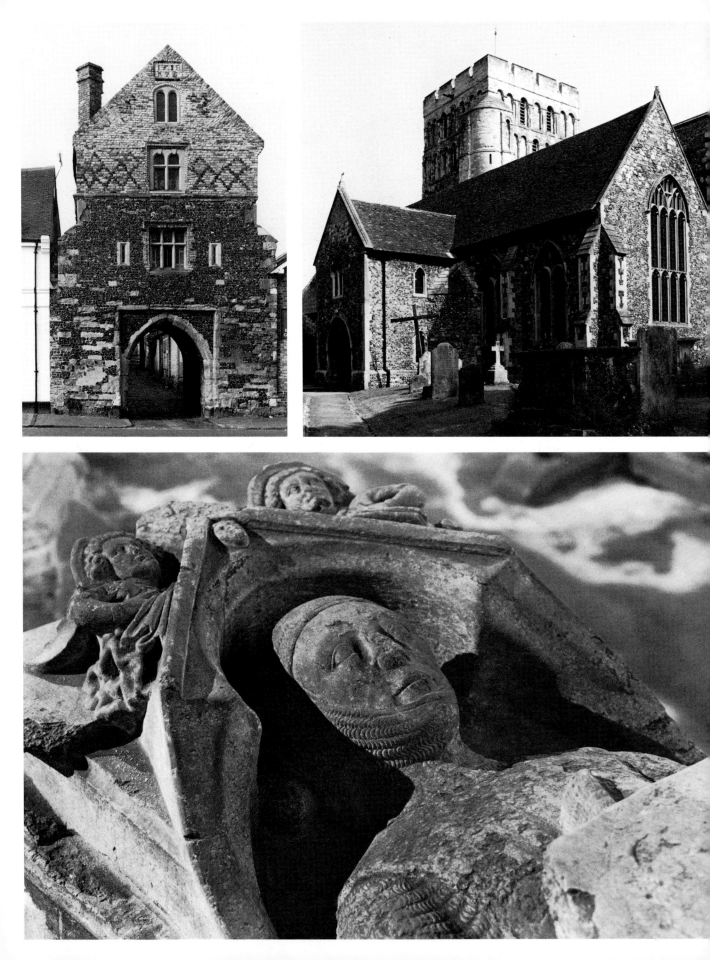

9 (right). *Delf House, 21 Delf Street*

10 (far right). *Horse Pond sluice, Delf Stream*

6 (far left). *Fisher Gate*

7 (left). *St Clement's Church: tower*

8 (left). *Knight's effigy, St Bartholomew's Hospital chapel*

So what remains prior to this second assault by the French? Not very much. The principal survivor is the tower of the parish church of St Clement (7). This imposing structure, of Caen stone, built by the Normans, emerged unscathed from both the French raids. It is a central tower, with a robust stair turret at the north-west corner, and the only Norman relic in Sandwich of any artistic importance. The date is about 1140–50.

About a century later was carved the finest piece of sculpture in Sandwich: an effigy, remarkably well preserved, in the otherwise drastically Victorianised chapel of St Bartholomew's Hospital outside the ramparts (8). The Knight, perhaps Sir Henry de Sandwich, who died about that time and was a great benefactor of the hospital, is clad from top to toe in chain mail, including a coif to protect the head. The material is one of those limestones so full of fossils that they will take a polish, and so in England pass for marbles. The nearest of these stones to Sandwich was at Bethersden, near Ashford. Whether this is Bethersden, or Sussex marble from near Petworth, or Purbeck, still farther away but accessible by sea as the other two were not, is uncertain. The execution is most accomplished, and specially charming is the boldly carved trefoiled canopy surrounding the head, which is surmounted by a pair of delightful angels.

Another survivor from at least as early as 1200 is the canal known as the Delf Stream. Although when one looks at it today it seems difficult to believe, this narrow canal (10) was in fact, right on until 1894, the town's sole source of drinking water. It was no good sinking wells here, for the town is practically at sea level. They had to tap a stream a couple of miles away to the south and construct a channel, which had to be lined with stone. Unfortunately, most of this water has now been diverted to serve the needs of industry; but the channels are still there, some underground, others exposed. So a number of houses are still entered across little bridges (9).

11. *The former Grammar School in Strand Street, now Manwood Court*

12. *5 King Street*

The twofold disaster of the French raid of 1457 and the gradual silting up of the Haven led to a sad decline. The population fell by three-quarters: from 3200 before the Black Death to a mere 800 or so by 1550.

What saved the situation, in the second half of the sixteenth century, was a sudden influx of Netherlanders fleeing from the oppression of Philip II of Spain. Queen Elizabeth welcomed them, and many of them settled where they had landed, here in Sandwich. By 1582, when Sir Roger Manwood's Free Grammar School (11), with its five crow-stepped gables in the Flemish mode, had just opened, there were nearly 400 of them, and a generation later there are said to have been more Netherlanders living in Sandwich than there were Englishmen.

They were weavers, producing in particular serges and flannels, and, as today, enthusiastic gardeners. It was they who introduced market gardening into England.

They also left their mark upon the town's architecture. They built with so-called Dutch bricks, which are much smaller than ours: they only measure $6-7'' \times 2\frac{1}{4}-3'' \times 1\frac{1}{4}-1\frac{1}{2}''$. Good specimens can be seen in King Street, at No. 5 (12) and No. 7, and especially at No. 62, which is known as The Old Dutch House (13). Leaving aside the blocking of the right-hand doorway and the later windows (a change, it may be felt, for the better), this has a complicated elevation which is not, I feel, very successful. It is too 'busy': too much is going on. But it is an interesting piece of brick craftsmanship. What a pity that at a later date it was whitened.

13. *The Old Dutch House, 62 King Street*

14. *Sandwich looking towards St Peter's Church*

A much more pleasing example of the Dutch legacy is seen in the presence here of pantiles (14). These were not made in England until the beginning of the eighteenth century, and when they are earlier than that they were always imported from Holland. They are not at all common in the South-East, but

Sandwich, presumably because of its long-standing links with Holland, has quite a sprinkling of them: and very delightful they are.

But so are plain tiles, which can often be seen to perfection in the south-eastern counties. Sandwich has a profusion of beautiful roofs of hand-made tiles, glorious alike in colour and texture. A very large one, of the finest quality, covers the south aisle of St Clement's (15).

After 1648, when the Treaty of Münster finally released the Netherlands from the rule of Spain and secured their independence, some of the immigrants returned home. Sandwich, no longer a port, went through another lean period, and probably looked rather down at heel. Although it still sent two members to Parliament, Defoe in 1723 found it 'old, decayed, poor and miserable', and a generation later John Wesley spoke of 'poor dry dead Sandwich'. Some of the inhabitants resorted for a living to smuggling.

So, unlike Cirencester or Bury St Edmunds, there is not much here of Georgian elegance. There are very few houses which, like several in Fisher Street (16), are completely Georgian. On the contrary, the typical Sandwich house is timber-framed. Indeed, the south-west side of Strand Street (17) is said to possess the longest continuous run of timber-framed houses of any town in England.

15. St Clement's Church from the south-west

17 (right).
*Looking along
Strand Street*

16 (left). *28
Fisher Street*

This is not to imply that the timbers are still exposed; in the majority of buildings they are not. But what we find wherever we go in this town is the jetty: the projecting upper storey (19). That is an infallible indication of a timber-framed structure. Sometimes the ground floor was built out later, to bring it flush with the face of the storey above and secure more accommodation downstairs, as at 3–5 Vicarage Lane (18), a house which incidentally incorporates an arched doorway of stone which cannot be later than the thirteenth century. The building out would usually be done in brick, which would often then be rendered or, as here, whitewashed.

Once the timbers have been plastered over, it is not usually a good idea to expose them again, although this is still a popular practice. The reason is that the plaster covering, which is rather heavy, is normally supported on laths, and if these are later removed, as has occurred at No. 3 The Butchery (23) (a house with a nice late-Georgian shop-window), the oak studs, as they are called, are left riddled with nail-holes, which do not look well at all (21).

Aesthetically, however, the trouble with framed houses whose timbers have remained exposed is that they have hardly ever escaped considerable, and often drastic, restoration. Sandwich provides far more examples than can be illustrated here. One of the commonest, and worst, faults is the introduction of badly designed and wholly unsuitable windows (22), which is specially distressing when, as at Nos. 13–15 Strand Street, most of the fifteenth-century

18 (right). *3–5
Vicarage Lane*
19 (far right).
*15–21 Church
Street St Mary's*

23 (above). *3 The Butchery*

24 (right). *Carving of a Centaur, King's Arms, Strand Street*

20 (top left). *39–41 Strand Street*

21 (far left). *Nail-holes in studs, 3 The Butchery*

22 (left). *13–15 Strand Street*

oak framing has survived in excellent condition. At Nos. 39–41 (20) only the robust timbers on the first floor are partly genuine; but what could look more inept than the modern windows cutting right through all but one of the braces? It is good to realise that such treatment as this could not be meted out today on a house, like this one, which is scheduled.

There is not much ornamental carving on the timber-framed houses at Sandwich, although in the centre of plate 22 can be seen the right half only of a late fifteenth-century doorway with lively carving in the spandrel. (The other half was destroyed in making the shop-front: something else which would certainly not have been permitted now.) The most enjoyable wooden figure is the Centaur on the corner post of the King's Arms, facing St Mary's Church (24). The date is there: 1592. It is sad that – comparatively recently, for old photographs show it *in situ* – the poor creature has lost his nose. The shock of hair strikes a wholly contemporary note.

25. *The King's Arms*

The inn itself (25), with its pretty windows, is jettied on both its exposed fronts but wholly rendered, and surely the better for it. Additional support is given to the jetties by a succession of carved brackets, but their function is primarily ornamental. Sandwich abounds in jettied structures with no brackets.

There is an air of improvisation about some of these old framed houses which can be rather endearing. Malt Shovel House in Delf Street is basically fifteenth-century, although much altered. When the building was refronted in the eighteenth century the man who inserted a new door (26) clearly had a sense of humour!

The practice of removing the plaster infilling and substituting bricks – what is known as brick nogging – became increasingly common in English timber-framing, as can be seen to good effect in Church Street St Mary's (27). The intention was to make the houses warmer, but this did not always succeed, because the weight of the bricks was likely after a while to cause the timbers on which they rested to sag, thus producing new apertures at the top of each panel. Often, as at The Old Drum, the bricks were set diagonally, in herring-bone fashion. A few doors away, Nos. 28–32 (28) exhibit other patterns of nogging besides herring-bone.

Unfortunately, however, most of this brickwork has been whitened. The aesthetic propriety of painting or whitewashing brickwork is controversial. A house faced with Victorian machine-made bricks arranged in polychrome patterns may cry out for a coat of good paint to mask them. But it must be

26 (right). *Malt Shovel House, 17 Delf Street*
27 (far right). *The Old Drum, 22 Church Street St Mary's*

28 (right). *28–32 Church Street St Mary's*

29 (left).
*Blenheim House,
36 Delf Street*
30 (above). *24–26
Millwall Place*

recognised that, once done, you are committed: you will never really be able to get it off again. So great caution is required, and the better the bricks, the less is the justification for covering them. Kent has made some of the finest bricks in England, and in this county painting or whitewashing is usually quite unwarranted.

Sandwich has a lot of brickwork treated in this fashion: in my view a good deal too much. Blenheim House in Delf Street (29) is an old timber-framed house which was refronted in brick in 1709. Later the ground floor was rendered. Today the entire building is decked out in *eau-de-nil*, which provides a 'tasteful' background, no doubt, for the white-painted woodwork, but is it kind to the brickwork? One needs to raid the larder to describe some of the other colours to which Sandwich bricks have been subjected: strawberry ice cream, vanilla, French mustard, weak *café-au-lait*. Other colours include battleship grey and, of course, plenty of white. Haven House in Harnet Street (31), one of the town's best, is a framed building dating probably from Elizabethan times which was refronted in red brick in the Georgian period. Later, quite improperly, I would say, it was painted white. Now it is dark grey, which is perhaps better: but it ought to be red – and of course I do not mean painted red. The die, alas, has been cast. Moreover, the paint has now to be annually washed, and from time to time renewed.

Unpainted brickwork may look cruder; even the best cannot attain the urbanity of ashlared stone. Yet it is, surely, much more satisfying. A good deal here is not red but pale yellow or brown: the London stock brick, in fact, made at Sittingbourne and other places along the south side of the Thames estuary. In the Regency and early Victorian periods bricks of these colours were often preferred, as for the pleasant terrace of artisan houses (with all the glazing bars of their windows intact) in Millwall Place (30).

31 (top right).
*Haven House, 29
Harnet Street*
32 (right). *68
Strand Street*

33. *St John's Cottages*

Another very pleasing instance is No. 68 Strand Street (32), which is a refacing of an earlier, timber-framed structure. This apparently simple front owes a great deal to the gently inset arch of the doorway, to the lofty recessed panels framing the side windows, and to the broad projection of the cornice. No. 87 opposite, and of about the same date, is also brown in front, with red confined to the high-quality gauged window-heads. But at the side they did not mind using red bricks, which were locally made and cheaper.

St John's Cottages by the former Cattle Market (33) are of yellow brick, and the rubbed brick window-heads are also yellow, but red was introduced for the modillions of the eaves-cornice, preparing the eye for the delightful red roof of hand-made tiles. Built in 1805, these cottages were almshouses until about twenty years ago, when they were condemned by the old Borough Council as unfit for habitation and ripe for demolition. Private people stepped in, managed to have them listed, restored them beautifully for holiday letting, and created a garden in front. There is no better example of the 'caring spirit' displayed by so many people in this town.

Even when none was available locally, churches until the Georgian period were nearly always built of stone. Sometimes this had to be brought from a considerable distance, and I have already noted that the tower of St Clement is built of Caen stone from Normandy. Locally the only stone was chalk: lumps of it, including ragstone, which was quarried at Hythe and Sandgate, and flints, a product of the upper layers of the chalk formation, there for the gathering, from fields and also from the beaches below the chalk cliffs a few miles away to the north and south.

Sandwich has three churches, St Clement, St Peter and St Mary, and all

34. *St Peter's Church from the south-east*

35 (left). *Garden wall, 29 Harnet Street*

37 (right). *The Barbican*

36 (left). *St Thomas's Hospital (almshouses)*

38 (right). *Pellicane House, 22 High Street*

three are largely built of unknapped flints, interspersed with chalky lumps to produce an amorphous patchwork (34). It may well have been because of the indifferent quality of this stone that both the towers not built of Caen stone collapsed: St Peter's in 1661 and St Mary's seven years later. The former church had been handed over to the Dutch refugees, who rebuilt the tower almost immediately, but in buff-brown brick. The only clay to hand locally was the river mud, so this is what they used. No wonder the result is somewhat mean. This church is now vested in the wholly admirable Redundant Churches Fund and, though no masterpiece, is worth a visit. Lofty and light, the building gains greatly from being entirely bare of chairs or pews, revealing a lovely floor of polished stones, some very large, with a few black ledgers. The wooden roofs are striking, especially that of the north aisle, which is of a delightful complexity. It is sad that all they carry, externally, are modern machine-made tiles of morti-

fying monotony. On the other hand, the lead cupola of ogee form which crowns the tower makes a charming contribution to the Sandwich skyline (14).

St Mary has also been declared redundant. Here the tower was never rebuilt, and the church long remained derelict. It is still a melancholy old hulk, but not unlikeable: the one notable item is the late seventeenth-century timber roof, with tie-beams of considerable span, which until 1956 were entirely hidden from view by a low plaster ceiling. At St Clement too the roofs are internally the most enjoyable feature, especially that of the nave which has square panels and winged angels against the ridge beam. The Norman tower is internally somewhat obstructive, but its four arches are rather noble.

Apart from the churches, stone plays only a minor role in the architectural picture of Sandwich, and masoned stone is a rarity. It was occasionally employed in combination with flints to make a chequer pattern, as in Tudor times at the Barbican (37). (The upper part of this building is picturesque but quite modern. Until a few years ago it was a very irritating toll gate.)

Flintwork here can be good. In Harnet Street there is a garden wall which incorporates flints that have been both knapped and squared (35), a truly remarkable feat of craftsmanship for 1400 if, as the Department of the Environment declares, this is indeed their date. Elsewhere – for example, on the side wall of No. 82 New Street – can be seen flint cobbles, water-worn and no doubt gathered from a nearby beach, laid in level courses with yellow bricks at intervals: a Victorian sandwich, in fact, and quite nicely made.

But usually it must be acknowledged that flint builders at Sandwich could only produce a rather uninviting hodgepodge. The leading example is Pellicane House (38), which used to be known as Flint House and was formerly St Peter's Rectory. This is in origin a fifteenth-century timber-framed house, but nothing

Above, left to right:
39. *47 New Street*
40. *Richborough House, 7 Bowling Street*
41. *Wych House, 31 Fisher Street*

Opposite
Top, left to right:
42. *5 Bowling Street*
43. *46 New Street*
44. *50 King Street*
Bottom, left to right:
45. *52 King Street*
46. *48 New Street*
47. *34 St Peter's Street*

of that shows from the High Street, for it was refronted in the seventeenth century and much altered in the eighteenth and again in the nineteenth centuries. The small flints, much blackened and interspersed with re-used lumps of Caen stone and Kentish rag, are singularly unappealing. The impact of this house, with its five mysterious recesses (blocked windows?) on the first floor, is made despite, and certainly not because of, its materials.

Ragstone is a better colour, but otherwise almost equally unpleasing. St Thomas's Hospital (36) is a medieval almshouse rebuilt about 1850. Pretty well everything is wrong. Only the dressings are smooth. The walling is random and looks rather like crazy paving laid vertically: an aesthetic solecism and no mistake. The roof is Welsh slate, which is certainly not right for Sandwich. The chimney-stacks are faced with ugly cement rendering; one even carries a bright blue cowl! The barge-boards are heavy and coarse. Even the lattice grilles of the windows are so thick and clumsy that they must take quite a lot of light from the little rooms.

The scale of all these buildings is modest and homely. That is one's overall impression of Sandwich and there is hardly anything to disrupt it. Church Street St Mary's (28), the paths of which are paved with blue-grey bricks, is unusual in having a large tree and the corner of a church to provide a focal point. Usually there is nothing so big. Near the town centre there are streets which are still no more than ten feet broad: just wide enough, it is said, to accommodate the ox-carts which in earlier times had to thread their way down to the waterside. Many ancient passages also survive, though without the generic names – twittens, vennels, wynds, lanes, rows – applied to them at other towns which I have described. Holy Ghost Alley and Paradise Row are two of my favourites here.

Architecturally, therefore, the pleasures of strolling through Sandwich are unspectacular but cumulative. There is no grand building to steal the thunder. But among the small-scale delights nothing surpasses the Georgian doorcases. Not many people here, stuck with timber-framed houses, could afford complete Georgian rebuilding. So what quite a lot of them did was to clamp on a new Georgian front, the principal feature of which was the doorway. Not every Georgian doorway here belongs to an earlier house, but the majority certainly do. At Richborough House in Bowling Street (40), I would say incongruously, the later plasterwork has actually been cut away in a square above the doorway to reveal some of the late sixteenth-century timbers with brick nogging. Here the jetty also survives, with the hood of the Georgian doorway projecting beyond it. Three of the other doorcases illustrated (41, 42, 45) also belong to Georgian refacings of older houses. All have fluted pilasters, but the bolection moulded frieze in the entablature at Wych House (41) is unusual. Dentillated pediments are certainly more elegant.

48. *The Guildhall* Some of these doorcases have unexpected fanlights; at No. 34 St Peter's Street (47) it is of the butterfly type. But compared with the perfect proportions at Petersham House (44), it is evident that this one is too narrow. Proportions in Georgian architecture are a matter of infinite subtlety.

Doors at this time were almost always panelled. The usual door had three pairs of varying sizes, each panel being moulded and fielded (that is, with the central area raised), as in all the above examples except Wych House (41), where the fussy replacement with sunk panels is obviously much inferior. Panelled doors were also favoured in the early Victorian period, as at No. 46 New Street (43). At the adjoining house a modern door with glass panels has been substituted (46). This is always wrong, and can damage the overall appearance of a house quite seriously.

Nor did the Georgians ever use the 'bull's eye', the lump in the centre of a disc of Crown glass to which the glass blower's pipe was attached. In the eighteenth century this was always discarded, and the pair of bull's eyes at another house in New Street (39) go some way to spoiling what is in other respects a doorway of distinction. Nowadays, for some extraordinary and unaccountable reason, bull's eyes have become so popular in some quarters that they are even faked, as can be seen at No. 46 High Street and elsewhere in this town. Needless to say, they are completely anomalous: a *faux pas*, in fact.

A fake on a much bigger scale is the exterior of the Guildhall (48), one of the town's largest buildings. Originally Elizabethan, it was in 1812 encased in yellow brick. Exactly a hundred years later the external walls were completely

rebuilt. Parts incorporate old bricks and tiles, but unhappily there is also imitation timber-framing, blackened. Despite this, the interior is of some interest, especially the old Court Room, with panelling dating from 1607.

A substantial addition was made in 1973, at right angles to the earlier building. This was tactfully done and exactly right in scale: good bricks and tiles were used, and it was certainly wise not to continue with the timbering. This new wing also serves to mask the town's principal car park, which is always a good thing to do.

The grandest house in Sandwich – indeed, the only grand house – is, beyond question, The Salutation (49). This was not erected until 1911–12, on a site which, although within the ramparts, had managed to remain almost unbuilt over. One small part of it had formerly been occupied by the Salutation Inn, which explains the house's name.

The Buildings of England volume on East Kent, usually so perceptive, dismisses this house, surprisingly, as 'nothing but neo-Queen Anne', a judgment which seems to me to be a long way out. This is one of the major works of Sir Edwin Lutyens, who is now coming to be recognised for what he surely was: the greatest English architect of the last hundred years at least.

Lutyens's earlier houses were designed in an Arts and Crafts style derived from Norman Shaw, although far superior to any of Shaw's as works of art. But about 1906 he changed; always delighted by the geometry of architecture, his work now became more classical. On the entrance front (51), which faces west, this formality was carried through even to such a detail as the elegant flight of steps up to the door, with its wrought-iron balustrades which are very nearly quarter-circles. The debt, certainly, is to the Queen Anne style, yet no house in the days of that monarch was ever like this one.

The house is a big rectangular pile with a lower service wing on the north side. The three elevations, west, south and east, are all absolutely symmetrical. They are interrelated, yet quite distinct. The south front (49) is the least original, but so finely proportioned that it is extremely satisfying. The dormers, so often a weak feature, are beautifully handled here, with their hipped gablets and laced valleys. The tiled sides do not meet the roof at a sharp angle but are carried gently round on a curve: that is what is called a laced valley. It is sometimes found on stone roofs, but with tiles it is unusual: a typical Lutyens refinement.

Two factors serve to unite the three elevations: the materials – the fine bricks, with quiet reds and blue-greys judiciously mixed, the Portland stone dressings, the white-painted woodwork – and the skyline. The high-pitched roof with its dark-red tiles and the noble chimney-stacks are features which characterise Lutyens's earlier houses too.

49. *The Salutation*   On the east front (50), the windows to either side of the centre are arranged

The Salutation
50. *East front*

51. *West front*

52. *Gateway*

diamond-wise: an original feature, the appreciation of which is not helped by the invasive magnolias. Within, the planning is totally unlike that of any Queen Anne or Georgian house, and is full of subtle and delightful surprises.

The big garden, also designed by Lutyens, on axial lines despite an extremely irregular site, has had the benefit of rich alluvial soil deposited by the Stour in the days when that river was very much wider. The planting has often been ascribed to Gertrude Jekyll, with whom Lutyens many times collaborated. For this, however, there is no documentary evidence, and her recent biographer (Jane Brown, 1982) believes that the garden was probably not hers. But, she adds, it remains full of Miss Jekyll's inspiration.

The south lawn (49) is in intimate relationship with the parish church, the tower of which is a glorious incident in the view. Nothing in Sandwich is so consciously planned as this gorgeously extravagant house and garden, which for some years, until 1983, was regularly open to the public. The town has been much enriched by its possession.

After an alarming period when it was acquired by a developer who sought to destroy much of the garden and erect small houses on the site, for which planning permission was very properly refused, The Salutation now has a new owner, who, it is understood, intends to maintain it as it deserves. This is one of the very few twentieth-century properties to be listed Grade I.

At the main gateway (52) the architect displayed great ingenuity in linking an eighteenth-century cottage already on the site with a former stable building. Thereby he was able, in a typically original way, to capture in colour, in texture and not least in scale the essential character of Sandwich. The whole of the town within the ramparts, together with certain stretches of open land outside, has very properly been designated a Conservation Area. There are also the Sandwich Society, active in defence of the town's amenities, and a flourishing Town Scheme, launched in 1977. Requests for grants for renovation and improvements have been consistently high here, and in six years over £80,000 has been paid out, half coming from the Historic Buildings Council and the rest from Sandwich Town Council, Dover District Council and Kent County Council jointly. The by-pass road has also been an inestimable boon. Traffic in the narrow streets of this old town can still be bad, but it used to be well-nigh intolerable. The golf courses are two miles away, beyond the marshes, and do not impinge. The future for Sandwich looks bright, for there are so many people here who are determined that it shall be.

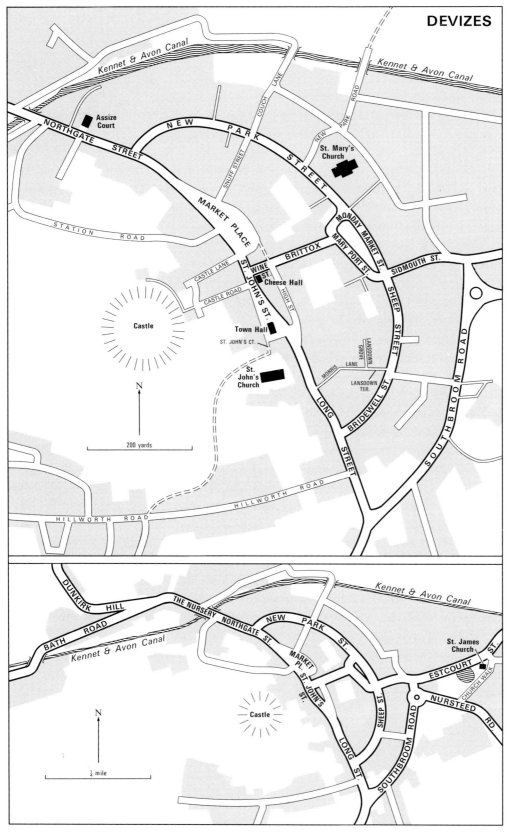

1. *Plan of Devizes*

DEVIZES

Wiltshire is a county spurned by holiday-makers. It has no coastline, and perhaps too many army training areas. Everyone seems to pass through this county on the way to somewhere else: to Somerset, perhaps, or Devon, or Cornwall. But not me: I like Wiltshire very much.

Devizes, which is almost plumb in the centre, is about 400 feet up on a spur of the Downs. To the west the land drops sharply, to yield tremendous views. In the other direction, on the chalk uplands above the Vale of Pewsey, are mile upon mile of fields, some under the plough, others just grassland, excellent for grazing sheep.

Devizes: what an odd name! Beloved, of course, by writers of limericks. It lines up with sizes, and prizes, and crops up in many disguises. The derivation is from the Latin, *ad divisas*, which means 'on the boundaries', and the story of this place starts with the erection of a castle by one of the bishops of Salisbury, probably early in the twelfth century, at the point where the boundaries of three manors converged. That castle, originally of wood, was rebuilt in stone in 1138, and after 1167 always belonged to the Crown. It was gradually left to moulder and decay until, after the bombardment by Cromwell in 1645, it was finally dismantled in the following year.

The site is occupied today by a pantomime re-creation of the Victorian period (2). It might have been done for William Randolph Hearst, but here a local tradesman got in first. Some of the windows aspire to be Norman, others Elizabethan. At certain points the ornamentation has an obsessive character. Elsewhere are genuine Norman bits, built into the garden walls. At one end is a big drum tower, and a lookout turret, also circular.

The castle is well built; part of the walling is ashlar, part coursed rubblestone. It is also very well situated, on top of a motte, surrounded by the driest of dry moats (4), a portion of which is now grazed by goats. Today there are rather too many trees and the grounds are a good deal overgrown, but it is remarkable to find this large private house (now divided), in its own grounds, within five minutes of the town centre.

The film-set character of the architecture is perhaps best appreciated at the entrance gateway (3), which has a toy fort aspect that is not unenjoyable. The coursed masonry, deliberately bold and rough, is rather effective. It is sometimes described as rock-faced.

To understand Devizes, one has to start with the Castle because the town grew up to serve it, and was planned in a segment of a circle below and around

it. The remarkable fact is that after over 800 years this street pattern still survives virtually intact (1). The streets run round in nearly concentric segments of circles. The ones furthest away were built first, because the nearer area was long occupied by the Castle's outer bailey.

But apart from the plan, very little survives of medieval Devizes except the churches, St John, St Mary and St James. All have good towers, but St James

2, 3, 4 (above). *Devizes Castle, gateway and moat*
5 (right). *St John's Church and Beauchamp Chapel*

6. *St James's Church*

(6), beautifully seen across the pond known as the Crammer, is otherwise all of 1832. St Mary (20) has a Norman chancel and a Perpendicular nave, but was much done over by the Victorians. St John is much the best of these churches; here the Norman inheritance is considerable, and strikingly evident in the central tower (5). This is rectangular on plan, with a prominent stair-turret at the north-west angle (48). Only the parapet and pinnacles are later. But the most gorgeous feature is the Beauchamp Chapel at the south-east corner (5), added about 1490 in the opulent manner characteristic of the Tudor period. This parapet is sumptuous.

The town itself at this time, like most others in England, was probably entirely timber-framed. Most of those flimsy houses disappeared a long time ago, but a few survive: more, in fact, than might be supposed, because some were later provided with new brick fronts.

A range of houses in St John's Alley is today looking very sorry for itself. Of about the same date as the Beauchamp chapel, it is humble indeed by comparison. The evocatively named Monday Market Street has the oldest surviving building, Great Porch House, of *c.* 1480 (7). This must have been a house of some importance, sited in what was the original market place. The windows were all altered in the Georgian period. The gable has a curved barge-board, unfortunately too much blackened now to be clearly seen. Barge-boards were both ornamental and functional, for they served to mask and protect from the weather the ends of the roof purlins as well as providing the gable itself with a pleasing finish.

The most – indeed, the only – enjoyable range of timber-framed houses in Devizes today is in St John's Court, at the entrance to the churchyard (8, 48). Built in the sixteenth century, and jettied throughout, these houses were also refenestrated in Georgian times. If the timbers were originally exposed, as I

7 (right). *Great Porch House, Monday Market Street*
8 (far right). *1 St John's Court*

9. *Elm Tree Inn, Long Street*

10. *26a–30 Long Street*

expect they were, they have long since been plastered over for greater warmth – and, the Georgians would have thought, for better appearance too. At No. 1, after the laths had decayed and the framework had been found to be riddled with death-watch beetle, one section was uncovered. This revealed that part of the infilling downstairs was brick, laid in herring-bone fashion. This has been left exposed. Although interesting in itself, it does not of course suit the unity of the rest.

The Elm Tree Inn (9) is a Jacobean timber-framed building which suffered the misfortune of being smothered with that most repellent of all building materials: pebble-dash. (Looking at it, I am reminded of the story of the Frenchman who was presented with a plate of porridge. He scrutinised it quizzically, then exclaimed, 'Very interesting, but what does one *do* with it? Does one *eat* it – or has one already eaten it?') Other changes – for example, to the windows – are more acceptable. Not long ago this inn, which has a delightful modern tiled roof, was smartened up with considerable flair. The pebble-dash is now *eau-de-nil*, a colour which provides an excellent foil to the profusion of white-painted woodwork.

In Tudor and Stuart times Devizes was not particularly prosperous. When William Camden wrote about it in 1610, he described the town as 'heretofore stately: now decayed and defaced'. It was just a small market town. Gradually, however, prosperity returned. Streets were given, and still carry, names redolent of trade: Wine Street, Snuff Street, Sheep Street. Sheep: they were what mattered most. In 1724 Daniel Defoe was able to record that 'the Devizes' – the prefix 'the', still common in French place names, was in general use here as late as this – 'is full of wealthy clothiers', engaged in the manufacture of 'mixed cloths, such as are usually worn in England by the better sort of people'.

The outcome was a massive rebuilding programme. Almost everywhere timber-framing gave place to brick, although sometimes only to brick fronts, as with some of the houses in Long Street (10). Gault clay, excellent for brick-making, was located not far away, and fully exploited. Devizes became, what to a large extent it still remains, a Georgian brick-built town.

11. *The market place in the early nineteenth century, from a watercolour by an unknown artist in the Town Hall*

In marked contrast with many other English towns, there was at Devizes plenty of room for expansion, on what had been the Castle's enormous outer bailey. So here in the course of the eighteenth century there gradually came into being the largest market place in the west of England (11). And a busy market it still is, every Thursday.

14 (above).
*Heathcote House,
Southborough
Road*
15 (right). *39
Long Street*

12 (left). *17
Market Place*
13 (left).
*Brownstone
House, 17–20
New Park Street*
16 (below).
*Cupid's head,
Brownstone House*

The Market Place contains a gallimaufry of buildings, to some of which we shall return. Not many here were built for private occupation. But No. 17 (12) certainly was: a handsome 'Wrenish' house dating from the early years of the eighteenth century. It is a pity that the doorway is off-centre, inevitable in a front with an even number of bays: but there is much to enjoy, from the Crown glass in the windows to the old tiles on the roof, which is hipped and sprocketed – swept out, that is to say, over the cornice. Stone is generously employed for the dressings: the door-frame with its broken pediment, the window architraves, the quoins, and the cornice with acanthus ornamentation on the modillions. Within, there is good plasterwork and panelling.

Undoubtedly by the same builder, and still finer, is Brownstone House (13) in New Park Street dated 1720. Except for a discreet one-bay addition on the left-hand side and the disposition of the chimney-stacks, this house is precisely symmetrical, which its style requires. All the dressings, again, are of limestone; the door is approached by five semicircular steps of diminishing radius, and surmounted by a jolly little cupid's head set against a pair of folded wings (16). But the brickwork here is of specially fine quality too: all deep-red rubbed bricks with very close joints. The windows, with their thin glazing bars, were, as at 17 Market Place, evidently renewed at the end of the eighteenth century. With craftsmanship of such distinction the new roof, of harsh machine-made tiles, comes as a nasty shock: surely a piece of false economy. This house is occupied by the County Council, so most of the rooms are now offices. The best feature of the interior is the staircase, with strong newel posts and 'barley sugar' balusters throughout: a considerable pleasure.

The forecourt wall, with a moulded stone coping, embodies rusticated stone piers carrying balls set within pedestal bowls, while at the centre there are panelled gate-piers with enormous cones as finials. With these the delicate wrought-ironwork of the gates provides a graceful contrast. At the back there was a large garden and a spacious stable block. This was obviously the house of a very successful man.

A more modest building of about the same date is Heathcote House (14) in Southborough Road. Here the windows are grouped in pairs, and preserve their original glazing bars, very different in effect from that in the 1786 addition just visible on the right. The modern roof, of so-called Double Roman tiles (that is, with two rolls rising from a flat surface), is rich in texture.

The pageant of good Georgian houses in red brick continued throughout the eighteenth century and beyond. Space will only permit the inclusion of a few more examples here. In Long Street alone there are at least a dozen good ones. Most of them happily retain all their glazing bars intact; No. 39, impeccably maintained, is the Rectory (15). Here the windows are set within architraves not of stone but of wood, very slightly recessed. The brickwork of the window-heads is gauged and rubbed. The dormers have casement windows with leaded lights. The roof of this house originally had limestone slates, which are unusual in Devizes. It now has pantiles, probably from Bridgwater. The good Tuscan porch is crowned by an attractive balustrade.

17 (top left). *10 Long Street*
18 (left). *Northgate House*
19 (above). *40 St John's Street*

At No. 10 (17), nearly opposite, the roof is of Welsh slate, but is not seen thanks to the (renewed) brick parapet. There is no porch, but the door is capped by a pediment resting on carved stone brackets. The architraves of the windows (all with their original glazing) are again stone, but their spacing is subtly varied.

Northgate House (18), now the Municipal offices, used to be the Judge's Lodging. Stone was employed here for all the dressings, including the moulded

20. *The Castle Hotel, New Park Street, and St Mary's Church*

cornice and the handsome Ionic portico approached by three stone steps. The later addition on the right, with canted bay windows of quite a different character, obviously does not belong and is to be regretted. The interior retains some good eighteenth-century fireplaces.

The late eighteenth-century Bank building on the corner of the Market Place and St John's Street (19), although basically brick, has the whole of the ground floor faced with stone and stucco, rusticated and partly vermiculated: a somewhat flamboyant Victorian alteration which enriched the building but did not improve it. The prominent keystones at every level are good.

Keystones are a characteristic of the Castle Hotel (20), also dating from near the end of the eighteenth century. This is in a more relaxed style, suitable to a hostelry, with its canted corner and its mansard or double-pitched roof with very big slates. The Tuscan Doric porch could be a later addition. The good red brick and fresh white paintwork of the Hotel, with the limestone tower of St Mary's church filling exactly the right place behind, combine to provide one of the most enjoyable street pictures in the town.

Early in the nineteenth century came two brick terraces that offer a rewarding contrast. Lansdowne Terrace (21: not easy to photograph) has some charming features: stepped stone heads to windows with all their delicate glazing bars intact, and, at second-floor level, plaques with graceful swags and rosettes. The weakness is at the top. The eaves are mean, and the top-storey windows are rammed right up against them: always a bad feature. A parapet would have looked much better here.

Lansdowne Grove (22, 23), which runs at right angles and stands within a large shared garden, has greater amplitude. Its origin was rather more classy. There are four houses, built, or so it is said, by the second Marquess of Lansdowne to house his four maiden aunts. Here the glazing is differently designed, and is no longer Georgian. This is what is known as marginal glazing. I do not like it as much. But the eaves are far more satisfactory than on the Terrace.

The special attraction here is the wrought-ironwork. Each house has an arched porch preceded by a scrolled overthrow. The lower balconies have interlaced arches and small quatrefoils, but on the upper floor are balconies of the scroll and honeysuckle pattern, much loved in England in the reigns of George IV and William IV. Nos. 1 and 2 have painted their ironwork white, Nos. 3 and 4 black. Which is to be preferred is a nice question. The white ironwork is more sparkling, but is it not also somewhat 'busy'? The black must certainly look better when viewed from inside, against the light.

Devizes has no stone in the immediate neighbourhood suitable for building. The nearest was at Westwood, close to Bradford-on-Avon; there was plenty more near Limpley Stoke, a few miles farther on. Stone from these quarries, which all belong to the Bath group, could be brought up the Avon to Melksham

21. Lansdowne Terrace (on right) and 1 Lansdowne Grove

22 (above). *3–4 Lansdowne Grove*
23 (right). *1–2 Lansdowne Grove*

without difficulty. But although only seven miles away, Melksham is 300 feet lower; thus there would have been a long uphill haul at the end of the journey. In 1810 this problem was to be solved by the opening of the Kennet and Avon Canal. Nevertheless, in addition to the medieval churches, there are in the town a number of stone, or at least stone-faced, buildings which antedate the construction of the Canal.

One of them is Parnella House in the Market Place (24), dating from about

24. *Parnella House, 23 Market Place*

1740. It is nothing if not provincial: ham-fisted, in fact. The Venetian windows on the first floor really make no sense at all. The raised centre of each has to be blocked, to accommodate the floor of the upper storey. How inept too is the (renewed) statue of Aesculapius, the son of Apollo and the god of medicine, in the niche. But the man, presumably a doctor, who built this house had classical pretensions, and he wanted a screen of columns; so stone was obviously very desirable here. From the direction of Bath it was duly obtained.

Sandcliffe, in Northgate Street (25), has a façade that is less original but very much more successful. This is an early Georgian brick house faced with Bath stone, as is clearly seen in the picture. The original windows were replaced by more elegant ones, perhaps about 1800. They retain their Crown glass. Here the chimney-pots have wisely been removed.

Also belonging to the group now being considered is the most popular building in the town, the Bear (27), which has been the leading hotel here for over two hundred years. ('What would Devizes be without the Bear?' they ask. And the answer is – wait for it – 'UnBearable!') The landlord here in the 1770s was the father of the future Sir Thomas Lawrence, the great painter of the time of George IV. The precocious little boy would earn some honest pennies by tossing off portrait drawings of some of the guests.

The Bear comprises two distinct buildings which have next to nothing in common. The earlier of the two is the right-hand one, which was originally timber-framed and erected in the late sixteenth or early seventeenth century; it has comparatively low rooms. In the time of Queen Anne it was refronted, and the coupled windows on the first and second floors are of this time. During

25 (below). *Sandcliffe, Northgate Street*

26 (right), **27** (bottom). *The Bear Hotel, Market Place, with detail of window*

the Regency this front was faced with stucco and given its grandly self-confident gilt lettering.

But much more distinguished architecturally is the left-hand part. The side elevation of this is brick, but the front, with its broad canted bays dating from the reign of George III, is entirely faced with Bath stone. At each end are slender Ionic pilasters, half oval on plan, and reeded with the greatest delicacy. There is reeding too along the frieze below the cornice and even on the edge of the coping of the parapet. Most unexpected of all, both for its glazing and for its architrave, is the central window (26), flanked by medallions with flowers and hanging garlands. The carving here is as crisp as when it was first executed, two hundred years ago.

Less unexpected is the use of stone in the Georgian period for facing buildings of a public character. Such was the Cheese Hall (28), erected under George II. This also served for a while as the Town Hall, and later as a laundry, and from 1836 to 1956 it was the premises of a wine merchant, for it has extensive cellars. The market for cheese, butter and eggs occupied the ground floor, which

28. *The Cheese Hall, Wine Street*

was originally open. Another name for the building is the Clock House. The site had previously been occupied by the Wool Hall.

This is not a skilful building. An architect who knew his classical grammar properly would have had three windows on the front or five: not four. When four windows are, as here, divided by engaged columns, one of the latter has to be exactly under the apex of the pediment, which is wrong: it turns the elevation into what is known as a duality. None the less this building, which is entirely faced with Bath stone and prominent in the view from the Market Place, is by no means without its attractions. The rusticated arches provide an excellent base for the smooth ashlar above, while the sculpture in the pediment, though not all well preserved, has much charm. The clock, set within a wreath and capped by the town arms, is flanked by a pair of cupids and by leafy scrolls. Very much to be deplored is the bright, electrically-lit sign advertising the Building Society.

A hundred yards or so beyond is something far more accomplished: the Town Hall (29) of 1806–8. For this not only was the facing stone brought

29. *The Town Hall*

from Bath but the architect too: Thomas Baldwin, who was responsible, as Surveyor, for some of that city's most important works. His Town Hall, a remodelling of an earlier one, is surely the gem among the buildings of Devizes, a work of the utmost grace and refinement, and with first-rate masoncraft. Here too the ground floor was originally open – and was also once a cheese market; the three segment-headed windows, with too much white woodwork, are the one feature which does not measure up to the high quality of the rest. Within there is, upstairs behind the handsome bow, an Assembly Room with an elegant Adamish plaster ceiling.

1810 was a memorable year in the history of Devizes, for it saw at long last the opening of the Kennet and Avon Canal (31).[1] Providing as it did the principal

The Kennet and Avon Canal
30 (left). *The Caen Hill ladder*
31 (top). *Couch Lane bridge*
32 (bottom). *The Pool*

[1] The smaller Thames and Severn Canal, with a tunnel over two miles long under the Cotswolds between Coates and Sapperton, had preceded it by twenty-one years, but suffered from a great inconvenience, a foretaste of the railways' 'battle of the gauges'. The locks on the east side of the tunnel were built to accommodate the Thames barges, which were long and narrow. On the west side they were shaped to suit the Severn trows (as their barges were called), which were shorter and broader. Hence at Brinscombe near Stroud all the freight had to be transhipped, which was both time-wasting and expensive.

link between London and Bristol, between the basin of the Thames and the Bristol Channel, this in its day was one of the great canals of England: the Great Western of the Canal Age. It had taken sixteen years to construct. The engineer was none other than the great John Rennie, a Scotsman by birth (like his equally eminent contemporary, Thomas Telford), who was soon to achieve fame for his Waterloo Bridge in London. The big challenge was the climb of nearly 300 feet from the Avon Valley to Devizes, necessitating the famous ladder of locks, the Caen Hill ladder. (The name, pronounced Cane, reflects the fact that during the Napoleonic wars French prisoners were held in this area.) Within $2\frac{1}{4}$ miles there are twenty-nine locks, only one fewer than the flight at Tardebigge on the Worcester and Birmingham Canal, the longest in England. On Caen Hill sixteen locks are contiguous (30). At present, unfortunately, they are derelict, and the large pounds to the side of each lock, which had to be filled with water pumped up from the Avon, are dry. But the Kennet and Avon Trust, a private organisation of canal enthusiasts formed in 1962, very much hopes to be able in due course to restore them.

Higher up, much good work has already been done. The Transport Act of 1968 divided the 2000 miles of canals which still remain in England into three categories: Commercial waterways, Cruiseways, and what were called

33. *Kennet Lock*

34. *The Town Bridge over the canal*

35 (far left). *Besborough Lodge (formerly Canal Lodge)*
36 (left). *Durleston (formerly Bridge House), Bath Road*

Remainder waterways. In its early days the Kennet and Avon Canal carried agricultural produce, stone and a great deal of Somerset coal, but no part of it is now 'commercial'. The Trust's aim, in collaboration with the British Waterways Board, is to recover as much as possible, and eventually the whole eighty-six miles, as a Cruiseway. From the Pool (32) at the head of Caen Hill ladder boats, after negotiating a number of more widely separated locks which have all now been restored (33), can continue for nineteen miles, to Crofton Top, south-east of Marlborough. For fifteen miles there are no locks at all.

It was of course, here as elsewhere, the coming of the railway which finally killed the canal. The Great Western Railway bought it in 1851 on the condition that it would be maintained in a navigable state. It was found to be increasingly unprofitable and more than one attempt was made to close it. But even after the last war it was still navigable, if only just.

In its heyday all the places through which it passed benefited greatly, and not least Devizes. After 1810 Bath stone began to travel as never before, and incidentally became one of the least expensive limestones in the country. To Devizes, which was on the direct route, it could be brought with no difficulty at all, so after the opening of the canal the number of stone-faced buildings rapidly increased.

An obvious user was the Canal Company itself. It had to build the Town Bridge (34) at the west end of Northgate Street, and this is entirely of ashlared Bath stone. The three-centred arch spanning the waterway is neatly echoed by the similar but much smaller one over the towpath. On the bank above is Besborough Lodge, the house originally provided for the lock-keeper (35), and even for this modest little building Bath stone ashlar was employed throughout. It is to this that it owes much of its appeal. Half a mile farther west, close to the Pool, is a larger Bath stone house, now called Durleston (36), which may also have been erected for a lock-keeper; it was certainly connected with the canal. It has an Ionic porch.

So has The Cedars, Bath Road (37), now the offices of Kennet District Council. This seems to have been built, perhaps before the opening of the canal (the exact date is not known), by some prosperous local tradesman, in

37. *The Cedars, Bath Road*

its own grounds on the outskirts of the town. Its chief appeal today resides in the superb quality of its masonry. It is worth comparing the almost invisible joint lines of the main wall with the all too obvious ones of the parapet, repointed recently. The art of fine pointing seems, alas, to have been lost.

Almost opposite is Trafalgar Place (38), a range of five houses dating from 1842 which were intended to form part of a terrace; but this was never completed. The Bath stone ashlar is again of the highest quality. The ground floor has banded rustication. The windows, which have kept all their glazing bars, are all four lights wide, but diminish in size at each storey. One house, and so far one only, has been discriminating enough to sweep away its farrago of undignified chimney-pots.

Close by, and of about the same date, is an unusual little building known as Shane's Castle (39), which was originally a toll-house. A rectangle with canted corners and an octagon with what was formerly a projecting porch have been ingeniously integrated. Here the Bath stone masonry is what is known as range work. The stones, which, though smooth and carefully coursed, are all small, are sometimes called ashlar bats. They were made from the smaller quarry blocks and from offcuts. No builder liked to waste his offcuts, so when work was slack the men would be put on to cutting these up and trimming them. They sold for less than the larger blocks, but were perfectly suitable for small buildings like this one.

Bath stone has always been notable for the ease with which it can be carved when first quarried; like all the limestones, it has the convenient property of hardening upon exposure to the air. In the Market Place No. 40 (40), dating from 1866, displays, in addition to excellent ashlar, a great deal of carved ornamentation. Ruskin's *Stones of Venice* had been published in 1851-3, and that is surely where we should look for the source of this thoughtful design. There is, so far as I know, no building like this in Venice, but I feel that there might have been. The gabled doorway, the oriel window, the shafts with leaf capitals framing the door and each of the first-floor windows, the profusion

of carved foliage, the small heads: all these are redolent of the age of Gothic. Other features, such as the sheet glass of the windows, are of course unmistakably Victorian. The design of the modern shop-front is sensitively in tune with the rest. Pevsner termed this building 'sweetly debased'. Maybe: but in its way it is quite a treasure.

For public buildings, needless to say, stone, and always Bath Stone, was now employed as a matter of course. Nowhere is this fine material seen to better advantage than at the old Assize Court (41), erected in 1835 in a very imposing Grecian style by T. H. Wyatt, before he was converted to Gothic. Here is expressed the full majesty of the Law, and no mistake! It still houses the Law Courts and the County Police Office. Slightly earlier (1830) and in a similar style is 41 St John's Street (42), with a rusticated base, and fluted columns to convey a somewhat more radiant and less forbidding mood.

The Market Hall (45) is a long narrow building dating from the same year as the Assize Court. The front is plain but dignified, with a well-designed clock tower. Directly in front of it, in the same stone but in a very different style, is the Market Cross (43), a well-proportioned and very successful essay in Perpendicular Gothic, which in fact preceded the Market Hall by over twenty years. It was designed by Benjamin Dean Wyatt, the great James's eldest son, in 1814. The donor was Henry Addington, who had been the Member for Devizes, and who in 1801 succeeded Pitt for a short time as Prime Minister. This prompted the squib from George Canning by which he is today best

41. *Assize Court, Northgate Street*

Opposite
42 (top left). *41 St John's Street*
43 (top right). *The Market Cross*
44 (right). *The Corn Exchange*
45 (far right). *The Market Hall*

remembered: 'Pitt is to Addington as London is to Paddington.' By this time he was Viscount Sidmouth, and is said to have presented the Cross with some show of reluctance, in fulfilment of a promise that he had rashly made to the townspeople seventeen years earlier. At least it can be said that when it came to the point there was no skimping.

On the opposite side of the Market Place is the Corn Exchange (44), a robust if somewhat florid Victorian design, with an outsize statue of Ceres aloft. This was built in 1856, at a time when corn had replaced cloth as the most important commodity in the town's economy. The angle piers have banded rustication and are crowned by big, somewhat fanciful urns, which recur several times along the side elevation (47). But the condition of the stonework is by no means as good here. It must have come from a different quarry.

Painted and rendered surfaces do not hold a prominent place in the architecture of Devizes. With good clay for brickmaking so easily available, and, especially after the arrival of the canal, Bath stone too, there was no need for them. Such examples as do occur mostly belong to the late Georgian and Regency years, when even the best brickwork was no longer in fashion.

The Black Swan (49) was formerly a coaching inn: an attractive brick building dated 1737 on a rainwater head. Some time later all the brickwork was limewashed. The present livery, white and grey, is not unpleasing, but probably no improvement on the original. Three years later a pair of brick houses went up behind the Town Hall, at the corner of St John's Alley (48). The style here is more rustic, and all the upper windows are clearly original. Yet later, again, the brickwork was masked. Here a coat of stucco was applied first, before the whitewash, which can at least be said to harmonise very well with the timber-framed range described earlier.

Stucco of a more urbane character distinguishes the former town house of the Lansdownes in Long Street (46). It is an interesting sidelight on the condition of the roads, especially in winter before the days of Macadam, that, although his estate at Bowood was only eight miles away, Lord Lansdowne considered it worth maintaining a house in Devizes. (It was, incidentally, on part of the large garden that was built the terrace for the four maiden aunts referred to earlier.) This house was built of brick towards the end of the eighteenth century. It seems probable that it was not stuccoed until a generation

47 (below). *The Corn Exchange, Station Road elevation*

48 (below right). *21–22 St John's Street*

49 (bottom). *Black Swan Hotel, Market Place*

50. *Hillworth House*

later, when were added the graceful portico with paired Ionic columns, the plat-band with a moulded Greek key pattern, and the elegant windows, each, upstairs, with its delicately bowed wrought-iron balcony.

In the first part of the nineteenth century there was such a vogue for stucco that some people actually preferred it to stone. Hillworth House (50) may well have been an instance of this: a Regency villa, with wings added about 1840. It is a house of some distinction (and, for once, the conservatory is architecturally no eyesore).

To conclude this account of Devizes we will repair once again to the Market Place, where the architecture constitutes a kind of synthesis of much of what this town has to show, good and bad. There is, let me add, very little that is bad.

The Victorians disliked stucco, which they regarded as a 'dishonest' material, and went back to stone and brick. Lloyds Bank (51), built in 1892, is, to put it mildly, not a restful building, but the craftsmanship is outstanding. The dressings here are of Portland stone as well as Bath, and are lavishly applied to brickwork of really superlative quality, some of it rubbed and some carved, as it occasionally was in the times of Charles II and Queen Anne. The ornamental panels above the central windows and the floral swags and ribbons to either side are prodigies of carved brickwork.

Towards the north-west the Market Place narrows, and there, closing the view, is the Brewery (52), dating from 1885, and of red brick again. It is perhaps a little overpowering, but it is undeniably a building of character, and has, in my opinion rightly, been scheduled (Grade 2). What a relief not to find, on this important site, a towering block of flats or offices such as has done irreparable visual harm, for example, to Hoddesdon in Hertfordshire.

51. *Lloyds Bank, Market Place*

On the south-west side of the Market Place there is, at the time of writing, a gap. Should I say a rather *ominous* gap? I hope not, but look what happened a few years ago opposite, adjoining the Black Swan (49). That should be a lesson. About the replacement the authorities cannot be too careful.

And then there are those dreadful concrete lamp-standards (52), Betjeman's 'sick serpents'. What did the Market Place do to deserve them? Our steel industry, alas, is in the doldrums. Perhaps it would be a trifle less so if local authorities in Britain, like their counterparts in West Germany, would always insist upon having steel lamp-standards. Some concrete posts are now more acceptable than they used to be, but they are always too thick and, what is worse, they soon look drab and dirty. All modern standards, in my view, should be made of steel. We need many thousands of them. Concrete may be cheaper, but visually the cost of eyesores such as these is enormous. And they are specially offensive in Devizes because so much there is so good.

It has been said that this town got left behind in the nineteenth century because the Great Western Railway went another way. Later it got a branch line, but now, although it still has Station Road (47), it has no station: in fact, no railway at all.

Today, with a population of ten and a half thousand and a catchment area of a least twenty-five thousand, Devizes is a flourishing local centre at the very heart of Wiltshire. But although so centrally placed, it is not even the County Town, for which it was at one time in the running. Many may feel that it had a lucky escape.

52. *Market Place, looking towards the Brewery*

DURHAM

Let us be clear at the outset what is our concern. In 1974 the boundaries of the ancient City of Durham were much enlarged, to embrace the former local authorities (Urban District Councils) of Brandon and Byshottles and Durham Rural District Council, as well as Durham Municipal Borough Council. These outlying places hold little of architectural interest, which at Durham is concentrated on the historic City. This means the rock-girt peninsula nearly surrounded by the River Wear, the bridges, and beyond, the parts of the town closest to those vital links (1). For special reasons, two short excursions will be made farther afield, but two should suffice.

A great many people's acquaintance with Durham does not extend beyond the view from the train that follows the East coast route from London to Scotland; but that is already sensational enough. The railway at this point runs high, and the approach to Durham station from the south (in fact, here, from the south-west) is across a bold eleven-arched viaduct (2) 100 feet high, built in 1857. From here the views are unforgettable (3). What a sight! And what a site! The site explains why Durham is where it is. In troublous times the flat top of its precipitous rock, dropping sheer into the wooded gorge of the river on three sides and easily defensible on the fourth, was a place which could be rendered virtually impregnable. And thanks to the Scots it needed to be, for their attempts to conquer the North of England were incessant.

In the seventh and early eighth centuries Christianity threw up a number of famous figures in Northumbria and Mercia: Aidan, Cuthbert, Wilfrid of York, Chad of Lichfield, Bede. All but the last were canonised. Cuthbert was one of the first bishops of Lindisfarne or Holy Island, off the coast of Northumbria; and there in 687 he was buried. Nearly 200 years later, the place was attacked by the Danes. The monks exhumed the body and fled. After eight years of wandering, they reburied him at Chester-le-Street in 883. There he remained until 995, when under Bishop Aldhun the saint was moved again, six miles to the south, to the then virginal site of Durham. Bede – 'the Venerable Bede' – spent most of his life in the Saxon monastery at Jarrow, where he died in 735. Also for reasons of safety, his remains were transferred to Durham in 1022.

Accordingly, the Saxon cathedral became a place of pilgrimage, celebrated beyond any other in the North. But it endured for only about a century. The great Norman cathedral which mostly survives to this day was begun in 1093,

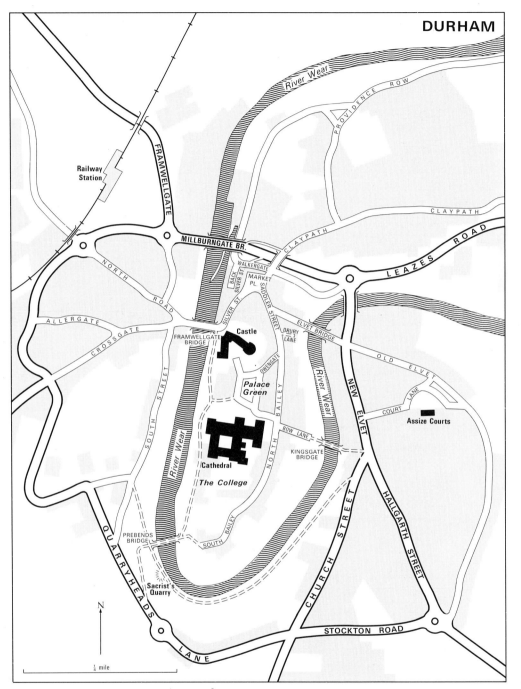

DURHAM

Railway Station

River Wear

PROVIDENCE ROW

FRAMWELLGATE

MILLBURNGATE BR.

CLAYPATH

CLAYPATH

LEAZES ROAD

WALKERGATE

BACK SILVER ST.

SILVER STREET

MARKET PL.

SADDLER STREET

ELVET BRIDGE

NORTH ROAD

ALLERGATE

CROSSGATE

FRAMWELLGATE BRIDGE

Castle

DRURY LANE

OWENGATE

Palace Green

River Wear

OLD ELVET

COURT LANE

NEW ELVET

Assize Courts

SOUTH STREET

River Wear

NORTH BAILEY

BOW LANE

KINGSGATE BRIDGE

Cathedral

The College

SOUTH BAILEY

PREBENDS BRIDGE

SOUTH

CHURCH STREET

HALLGARTH STREET

QUARRYHEADS LANE

Sacrist's Quarry

N

STOCKTON ROAD

¼ mile

1. *Plan of Durham*

2. The railway viaduct from the Castle roof

and forty years later, except for the towers, was virtually complete. Cuthbert was reinterred within a splendid shrine, and the pilgrimages gathered momentum.

The Norman rulers never lost sight of the need for strong defences. It was primarily because of their military efficiency that they survived. The conquest of Britain had proceeded so rapidly and so smoothly that before long only one adversary remained: the Scots. It was the recurrent danger from the North that accounted for the choice of Durham's site, for the strength of its defences and especially of its Castle, and for the exceptional powers vested in its bishop. The Bishop of Durham was the sovereign's representative in the Northern Marches: a terrific grandee. He had his own troops, his own courts of law, his own parliament; for a very long time Durham did not send any MPs to Westminster. He also minted his own coinage. And until 1565 he had absolute control over the town. It is not therefore surprising that both the Castle, where he resided, and the Cathedral were conceived on the grandest scale.

The builders did not have to look far for their stone: Coal Measures sandstone. The Sacrist's Quarry is only half a mile away, just across the river to the south. This supplied the stone for some of the monastic buildings – for the Cathedral was also the mother church of a Benedictine Abbey, served by half a hundred monks. But for the Cathedral itself this stone was not considered good enough, and another was selected. Kepier Quarry (4), in the woods above the Wear less than two miles to the north-east, has not been worked for centuries, but it can still be visited, and a very moving experience it is. Here, high above one of England's loveliest rivers, was hacked out the stone that was to give us one of our most glorious buildings; we cannot look at it, surely, without feelings of profound reverence.

Usually in the Middle Ages the stone for the cathedrals and other major buildings, unless (as at Lincoln) actually available on the spot, was brought to the site by water, in flat-bottomed boats. But the Wear at this point is not, and never was, navigable. It is too fast-flowing, and too full of rocks. So Kepier stone travelled overland, in carts hauled by oxen. There were steep hauls at each end of the journey which must have been very arduous; but otherwise much of the way was downhill.

It would be idle to pretend, however, that all the stonework here is now in good condition. Plate 5 shows part of the wall of the Deanery garden, adjoining the Cathedral. This is not, I think, Kepier stone, but the wall is old, and faces west: the impact of the weather is all too apparent. To expect any exposed stone masonry to escape decay after eight and a half centuries is perhaps hardly fair, although there are buildings which can pass even that test. Durham Cathedral is unfortunately not one of them. Needless to say it had no down-pipes, and in the course of time the sandstone became in places seriously eroded. So in 1777, on the advice of a local architect named John Wooler, instead of replacing badly-worn blocks with new ones, as is done today, they started chiselling away the entire surface to a depth of an inch, two inches: in places even three and more. This explains the somewhat rugged, untidy effect of much of the stonework, which is now a long way from smooth ashlar. And whenever there is a storm or a high wind, hunks of stone are still liable to break off and fall. In some places too it has, through air pollution, become almost black. But of course in varying degrees every cathedral has similar problems to face. For restoration work at Durham they now have to use Dunhouse sandstone, quarried near Barnard Castle. It is a good stone, and there are unlimited quantities available, but at first, inevitably, the new work does always look somewhat raw.

4. Kepier Quarry

5. Weathered stone in the Deanery garden wall

3. The Cathedral from the railway

The commanding features of the Cathedral's exterior are the towers, which are all immensely massive (6). None was carried up until the Gothic period, but the western pair (8) were completed quite early: probably about 1220. They show that aggregation of small effects – four tiers of comparatively small arches, some blind, some pierced – which is characteristic of Norman and early Gothic enrichment. None the less, they make a strong impact. From the fourteenth until the middle of the seventeenth centuries they carried lead-covered spires. I am glad that they do so no more. The present crowns date only from 1801, but are visually quite satisfactory.

The central tower (7) is a late fifteenth-century replacement after the old one, in 1429, had been struck by lightning and burnt. Aesthetically it has one serious defect: the top stage was clearly an afterthought. Just below the top belfry windows there is a rich parapet which was evidently intended to be the crown of the 1465 tower. The top stage added in the 1480s is too short; and why the builders, having decided on it, did not first remove the parapet and re-use it to crown their addition is a mystery. Nevertheless, this is a most majestic tower, and visually the resolve to go up higher, to 218 feet, was undoubtedly right. The building needs the higher central tower, just as surely as it does not need spires.

To step for the first time into Durham Cathedral (9) must always be, for

6. *The Castle and the Cathedral*

7 (opposite top). *The Cathedral from the south*
8 (right). *The west towers from the Cloisters*
9 (far right). *The nave*

anyone in love with architecture, one of life's most thrilling experiences. It will be impossible to do proper justice to it in what will have to be rather a brief account. Of all our Norman cathedrals this is far and away the best proportioned. Elsewhere the arcade tended in the twelfth century to be rather low in relation to what it carried. Here this is not the case at all: the arcade is

two and a half times the height of the tribune (the gallery above the aisles). The piers are of two kinds, circular and composite, employed alternately. The latter have a circumference of no less than seventeen feet. The circular piers have geometrical ornamentation – chevrons, spirals, diapers and vertical flutes – incised with unforgettable vigour.

10 (left). *Sanctuary knocker*
11 (above). *Flying buttresses in the triforium*

Most remarkable of all is the fact that this building, unlike any other English cathedral of the period, was vaulted from the outset. The choir vault, the earliest, had later to be reconstructed, but the transept vaults, dating from about 1110, and that over the nave, finished in 1133, have stood unscathed for over 850 years. How was this accomplished? It will help if we understand that a vault exerts two kinds of pressure: downwards, carried here by exceptionally massive piers, and outwards, counteracted by buttresses. Few people realise that this cathedral has flying buttresses, because they are inside, hidden under the aisle roofs (11). They were in fact the earliest flying buttresses in the country. To achieve greater flexibility, the Durham vault also has some pointed arches, nearly half a century before the arrival in England of the Gothic style of architecture with which these arches are usually associated. In this respect, too, Durham led the way.

Yet, with its slow, solemn rhythms the spirit of the building is still wholly Romanesque. So too is its ornamentation, with plenty of zigzags on the vault ribs (12), as also on the arches of the arcades at all three levels. All the vault ribs spring from corbel-heads carved with typical Durham vigour and zest.

This spirit can be captured again in the bronze Sanctuary knocker on the north door (10): a superb piece of stylisation. Initially the eye sockets were filled with coloured enamel, but in my view the disappearance of this is a positive advantage. The dark, cavernous eyes are surely much more evocative. (It must be added that this is no longer the original knocker, which, after restoration,

12 (right). *The nave*

13 (left). *The west front and the Galilee Chapel*
14 (above). *Chapel of the Nine Altars*

was wisely removed for safer keeping to the Treasury. The copy that replaced it on the door in 1975 is so true that hardly anyone would suspect that it is a substitute.)

Scarcely a generation elapsed before the Norman west door was enclosed by a Lady Chapel (13) known, for no very obvious reason, as the Galilee Chapel. It extends to the very edge of the precipice, which is why, in the 1780s, the Chapter proposed to demolish it in order to construct a drive pushing southwards past the west front. Fortunately this project was not carried out. Within (15), massiveness has given place to elegance. The piers are slender, the cross-vistas complex and fascinating, for here there are five aisles. No other cathedral has a chapel anything like this one.

At the other – the eastern – end, the cathedral breaks into the most exuberant Gothic. In 1242, to serve the purpose of the monks, the Norman apse began to be replaced by the Chapel of the Nine Altars (14). This formed a soaring addition to the building, where the stress is all on the verticals. The shafts of the wall arcade are of the local Frosterley marble, a limestone so full of fossils that, like Purbeck, it will take a polish. The one weak feature here is the rose window (9), which dates from about 1795. I call it the paper doily.

It has, like the chiselling of the external stone surface and the proposal to destroy the Galilee Chapel, usually been attributed to James Wyatt, but unjustly so. It was the work of his master-mason, who was instructed to copy the design of the old rose, which had decayed. Instead, he thought that he could improve upon it. As is evident, he was mistaken.

On the other hand, the Neville screen (17), installed in 1380, is a joy: surely the best Gothic reredos of any. This is not made from the local sandstone. It is of Caen stone from Normandy, and was carved in London and shipped up in pieces, all ready to be assembled. It was once filled with alabaster figures which have all vanished. I wonder how much this matters; the many openings are delightful.

Durham has few medieval furnishings, and for a very sad reason. After his victory over the Scots at Dunbar on 3 September 1650, Cromwell quartered some 3000 of his prisoners in the Cathedral. These poor wretches were incarcerated for many months without any heat whatsoever, so naturally they burned the woodwork in order to try to stave off pneumonia. It was Bishop Cosin who, after the Restoration, commissioned new stalls and a prodigious font canopy (16). This is one of only four canopies, as distinct from covers, in the entire country, and the largest: three yards across and over forty feet

15. *Galilee Chapel: interior*

high.[1] It is a pity that it is so black; and stylistically it is admittedly a hybrid:
Classical at the base, in harmony with the font itself, and becoming increasingly
Gothic as it climbs up. But the proportions are so felicitous, the silhouette

[1] The others are at Luton and in Norfolk: at Trunch and at St Peter Mancroft, Norwich.

17. *The Neville
screen*

18. *The College Gatehouse*

so successful, the surface enrichment so well managed, that we are much more disposed to admire than to cavil. This masterpiece of English carpentry is a work of such self-assurance that it is certainly no intruder into a Norman cathedral. In scale it is worthy of its setting. In every other aspect its success depends upon absolute contrast. In this canopy we have wood in a world of stone, mainly pointed forms in an *ambiance* of semicircles, delicacy and intricacy in the context of boldness and strength, and a light-hearted staccato rhythm to set against the solemn measured tread of Durham's superb nave.

Happily there is no risk of anybody attempting to emulate the conduct of those poor Scots prisoners today, for this is the best warmed of all our cathedrals; in winter there is even underfloor heating. And quite right too.

On the south side of the Cathedral is what is known as the College. This is

19. *Conduit (Well House)*

not a building but a precinct, and is in fact the Cathedral Close, surrounded by large houses which are all the property of the Dean and Chapter. They are of no special interest, but enjoyable none the less.

The only vehicular access is through a Gatehouse (18) built about 1500, with a chapel above. Within is a big lawn planted quite informally with small trees, around which the houses are ranged. Those on the west side have, at the back, spectacular views over the river immediately below. In front of these houses, in 1751, was erected, in the Gothick style, an octagonal Conduit or Well House (19); the designer may have been the amateur architect Sanderson Miller. Although no longer in use, its presence is still an ornamental asset to the lawn. Except when a waterfall of youngsters gushes forth from the Choristers' School in the far corner, the College is a haven of peace: one of the most secluded and delectable spots in Durham.

To enter the Cathedral from here, we pass the weather-beaten wall of the

20. *The Castle and Elvet Bridge*

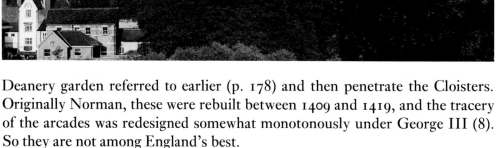

21. *The Castle from the north*

Deanery garden referred to earlier (p. 178) and then penetrate the Cloisters. Originally Norman, these were rebuilt between 1409 and 1419, and the tracery of the arcades was redesigned somewhat monotonously under George III (8). So they are not among England's best.

The other major occupant of the Rock is, of course, the Castle (20), which was for centuries the chief residence of the Prince-Bishops. This is a big building of many different dates, for throughout the centuries it was continually altered. Viewed from the north (21) we are impressed by little but its bulk, but at least it will be evident what a formidable face it presented to invading Scots or anyone else intent on capturing the lofty peninsula. This in fact never occurred.

The courtyard is entered through a Gatehouse (23) which is now much more consciously 'picturesque' than when it was originally erected by Bishop Le

23 (right). *The Gatehouse*

22 (below). *The Great Hall*

24 (bottom right). *The Black Staircase*

Puiset in the reign of Henry II. The elaborately carved archway is late Norman, but the rest is Gothick of about 1790: very enjoyable but quite unmilitary. Most of the west side of the Courtyard is occupied by the Great Hall (22), which is almost equal in size to the largest halls of the Oxford and Cambridge colleges. Little but the undercroft, however, is Norman. The much-restored

25 (left). *The Norman Gallery*
26 (above). *The Norman Chapel*

doorway dates from Bishop Cosin's time (1663), and so does the quartet of big buttresses crowned by ogee-shaped helmets. The interior is mainly Victorian.

In the angle between the west and north ranges Cosin inserted the Black Staircase (24), one of the most imposing in an age that was very fond of large, sumptuous staircases. The carving of the balustrades and of the facing dadoes is very rich indeed; it is said to be in willow wood. Some of the acanthus foliage sprouts from the mouths of wolves. The newel posts carry big vase-like ornaments with knobbed lids, inspired, to my eye, by artichokes. At the base of nearly every post is an unusual pendant. Only the Tuscan columns, inserted fairly recently for structural reasons, are to be regretted.

High up in the adjoining north range is a remarkable room of which there is no hint from outside, as the windows were Gothicised in the 1750s. Known as the Norman Gallery (25), this is, unfortunately now on the south side only, a rich and unique example of late-Norman architecture in a domestic context. The arched window embrasures, adorned with an abundance of chevrons, rest on slender columns and are flanked by window-seats.

From here a spiral staircase descends to the Norman Chapel (26), one of the very few in this country to have survived virtually intact from the eleventh century: the date is probably soon after 1080. Like the churches of the Anglo-Saxons, it is very tall for its area. The crude groined vaults are carried on six massive circular piers crowned by carved capitals of a lively but very primitive character. The prominent and attractive water-markings, which can also be seen in the south choir aisle of the Cathedral, are due to the presence of iron oxide, acting as a staining agent when the stone was formed.

On the east side of the courtyard rises the *motte*, a huge mound of earth thrown up in 1072 on the orders of the Conqueror, returning to London from Scotland. The big shell keep of stone which crowned it was not built until the fourteenth century; after the Scottish menace receded it was allowed to fall into a state of total dilapidation, which explains why the present structure (27) dates only from 1839–41, when Anthony Salvin was called in to provide accommodation here for students. Which brings me to the story of the foundation of Durham University.

After the Reform Bill of 1832 the richer cathedral foundations took fright. Parts of their endowments, they feared, were going to be confiscated, in order to pay for the building of churches in new urban areas. Durham was specially vulnerable, because its revenues – derived from agriculture, woods, quarries, lead and coal mines – amounted to over twice as much as those of any other cathedral. And ever since the time of Henry VIII the idea of creating a third English university, to serve the North, had been in the air: Durham was clearly a good place for it. The new University was founded in 1833. The Dean and Chapter took the initiative, but the Bishop was equally enthusiastic and generous – which he could well afford to be, since his revenues amounted to

27. *The Keep*

£19,000 a year. Four years later the Ecclesiastical Commissioners, at the suggestion of the Dean and with the full support of the Bishop, handed over the Castle to serve as the first college.

The University was therefore an ecclesiastical foundation: so much so, in fact, that at first the only subject that could be read was theology. For nearly a century it remained small, with seldom more than 500 students. So luckily there was no need to build big Victorian blocks.

Between the Castle and the Cathedral is a great lawn, Palace Green, that

28. *Palace Green and the Cathedral*

29. *Bishop Cosin's Hall*

30 (top left).
*Bishop Cosin's
Almshouses*

31 (top right).
*The former coach
house*

32 (above).
*University Music
School*

33 (right). *Abbey
House*

is sometimes mistaken for the Close, which it never was. Today the periphery is a strictly regulated car park, largely to serve the University; this is a pity but, I suppose, inevitable. At least it can be said that below the mighty mass of the Cathedral, which fills the whole of the south side of the Green, motor vehicles are dwarfed into appropriate insignificance (28). But the jingle of colours jars.

All the buildings bounding Palace Green now belong to the University. Architecturally they provide a very mixed bag indeed. Several are associated with Bishop Cosin, who brought the Cathedral back to life after its desecration during the period of the Commonwealth, and who was one of the See's most famous incumbents.

In the south-west corner is the old Grammar School, which is now the University Music School. This was founded in 1541 and rebuilt by Cosin in 1661. A century or so later, part of it was given a face-lift (32), but the chunky character of the uncoursed rubblestone (contrasting with the more recent restoration below the two right-hand windows) is a far cry from urban Georgian.

Across the Green, on its east side, are Bishop Cosin's Almshouses of 1668 (30), which now provide premises for the Union Society and for lecture rooms. Adjacent, to the south, and also of stone throughout, is Abbey House (33), a plain but gracious Georgian house which now accommodates the Department of Theology, now only one subject among many others.

At the other side of the Almshouses is the big early eighteenth-century house known as Bishop Cosin's Hall (29). In fact, the Bishop had nothing to do with it, for it post-dated him by several decades; it is so called because a University hall of that name occupied the house in the middle years of the last century. It is now divided into three spacious university flats. This house looks rather splendid from across the Green. Close to, it is not so good. We discover that the bricks are not of good quality, and that the lintels and aprons to the windows are faced with cement. The doorway too, which is not in the centre, even of its own bay, is really slightly ridiculous. This is early eighteenth-century building at its most provincial, remote from the work of the acknowledged architects.

Next door (31) is a little building which started life as the Bishop's coach house and stables. Salvin built it in 1841, while he was re-creating the Keep. Today it is a public lavatory, and few loos, surely, can hold their heads so high.

Round the rim of the little plateau which tops the Rock, extending for nearly

35 (right). *2 Owengate*

36 (right). *1–2 North Bailey*
37 (far right). *5 Owengate*
34. *The city of Durham in 1745*

a mile in all, ran – and in places still runs – a bracelet of ramparts (34), pierced by a number of posterns but by only one vehicular gateway, at the north-east corner. It comes as no surprise to find that nearly all the best houses in Durham, architecturally speaking, are within this *enceinte*.

Some of these also belong to the University now: 2 Owengate (35) is one of them. The whole of the back part of this house rests on what was once the perimeter wall of the Castle. Almost next door is the only house on the Rock still to reveal its original timber-framing (37): the double jetty, of course, gives the game away at once. But this house has been too much restored to be of any interest otherwise. We certainly do not visit Durham to see timber-framing.

The principal streets are North Bailey and South Bailey – one continuous street really, and the only one that runs along the whole length of the peninsula. The grandest house is 3 South Bailey (39), built about 1730 as the town house of the Eden family. This is exceptional in being stone-faced throughout, with banded rustication. There are not many stone-faced houses here, unfortunately. Brickwork in Durham, by the standards of the South-East, is not good aesthetically. Bricks made from the local carbonaceous clays (the only ones available) are usually durable, but quite devoid of charm. Often, too, there are patches of insensitive repointing (41, 42).

However, there are compensations. Most of the Georgian houses have retained their original glazing bars (40); their loss on the ground floor of Nos. 1 and 2 North Bailey (36) is immediately felt. Some of the doorcases are charming (41, 42). Doors of properties owned by the University, like Nos. 1, 2 and 39 North Bailey, are all painted turquoise blue. South Bailey has two visual advantages: it is winding, while North Bailey is almost straight, and most of it has kept its cobbles (38). Traffic here is light, as there is no exit for vehicles.

39. (right). *3 South Bailey*
40. (far right). *44–46 North Bailey*

41 (right). *39 North Bailey*
42 (far right). *6 South Bailey*
38 (below). *South Bailey looking south*

43. *Prebends' Bridge*

The Rock is joined to the 'mainland' beyond by four bridges across the elongated horseshoe bend of the Wear. Three of them entail steep descents; all four are now for walkers only. Two of these bridges are at the neck of the peninsula, Elvet (20) to the east and Framwellgate to the west. Both date originally from the twelfth century. Both have had to be much rebuilt after damage from floods, and in the cause of widening: but the work has been well done. Both are now good places to linger.

The original Prebends' Bridge, erected in the seventeenth century, was also damaged, indeed swept away, in the flood of 1771. It was replaced in 1772–8 by the present structure (43), the work of George Nicholson, the Chapter architect. It is undoubtedly the gem of Durham's bridges, beautifully masoned in the local sandstone, and embodying little subtleties such as the piercing of the parapet over the summit of each arch. I am not saying that level bridges like this one have quite the charm of those that rise a little towards the centre – bridges that are seldom built today, because of course they are very bad for traffic. But a lovely bridge this certainly is, and in situation altogether extraordinary. It appears to be in the heart of the country, yet is in fact only a few hundred yards from a busy town centre. Nothing is more astonishing about Durham, nor more fascinating, than the chance of having a peaceful woodland walk beside the river during the luncheon break.

Kingsgate Bridge (44) is very different, if only because, unlike the others, it is a high-level footbridge, spanning the gorge where the banks are at their

44. *Kingsgate Bridge*

most precipitous, which is a very great convenience for pedestrians. The views from it are almost unbelievably sylvan considering how close it is to the town centre. It was designed in 1962 by Ove Arup, and has been constantly commended. The ingenuity of its construction is famous: it was built in two halves, each parallel with its river bank. When both were ready, they were swung out through ninety degrees and locked together. As a work of engineering it is no doubt very successful. It is not, I submit, equally so as a work of art. The triangles which support it are not harmonious and unfortunately, having been constructed of concrete, it is already, after little more than twenty years, looking drab and down at heel. How much more visually satisfying would have been a leaping arch of steel: and with the great steelworks of Consett only a few miles away and then in full production, this would surely have been specially appropriate.

Beyond the bridges, there are not many buildings of high individual quality. The best are on the east side, in the quarter known as Elvet. Just across Elvet Bridge is the Royal County Hotel (45), of brick faced with stucco. This is basically Georgian, although a good deal marred by later alterations. But the front, with four very tall fluted Ionic pilasters, is still rather distinguished, and so is the lettering.

From here Old Elvet curves gently upwards. A hundred years ago this must have been Durham's finest street, wide and rather stately. The north side still

gives considerable pleasure. But alas, the south side was largely destroyed, first by the erection of 1896–8 of the old Shire Hall, in raw red brick with a green dome, both excruciatingly wrong here, and then in 1903 by the Methodist Church, with ugly rubblestone walls and a singularly graceless spire.

But it is worth continuing up the hill to see, set back on the right, the Assize Courts (now called the Crown Courts), completed in 1811. This is a long low building of considerable dignity: only the central portion appears in the photograph (46). The designer was Ignatius Bonomi, who, after John Dobson of Newcastle, was to become the leading architect in north-eastern England during the first half of the nineteenth century. The Durham Courthouse was his first work, completed when he was only twenty-four. It has greatly benefited recently from cleaning and restoration.

Throughout the Victorian period the town remained remarkably small and compact, with very little in the way of industry. In 1911 the population was still only 17,550. But since 1950 great changes have taken place. Far and away the most important architectural additions since then have been in connection with the expansion of the University. In the hilly area to the south there are now no fewer than six new colleges, as well as several faculty buildings and a distinguished Museum of Oriental Art. The primary reason for the construction of Kingsgate Bridge was to provide a convenient link between the new parts of the University and the older buildings on the Rock.

It is to see the new colleges that I make the second of my two excursions away from the vicinity of the Rock. They are all some distance out, but three of them have magnificent views of the Cathedral. First came St Mary's, a women's college, and the only one in a traditional, classical style. This was expensively built, and the main block, faced with sandstone, is certainly handsome, but architecturally very unadventurous for 1952. The other five all had to be built on a limited budget, and concrete bricks, of various shades, are the rule. All are by different architects, and vary considerably in character. The two latest seem to me to be the two best. Trevelyan College (47), also for women only, has no view, but achieves the most truly collegiate atmosphere. This is built of grey-brown bricks and is a subtle composition in interrelated hexagons, with an attractive layout. Collingwood, on the hill above, is more austere (48). The concrete bricks, predominately brown with hints of pink and grey, produce a mottled effect. The long ranges of students' rooms splay outwards to encompass a country view of great enchantment, without another building in sight. Collingwood College stretches out its long arms and seems to draw the landscape within their grasp.

The worst building of the post-war years is Millburngate House, erected in 1965–9 above the west bank of the Wear to accommodate the National Savings Bank. This assertive lump of hideous concrete could only have been put up by a Government department, exempt (as it should certainly not be) from obtaining planning permission; and it is a disgrace. If it had to be in Durham at all (and, surely, another more suitable town could have been chosen?), it should have been sited well away from the town centre. On the other hand,

46. *The Assize Courts*

the new Millburngate Shopping Centre, built in 1972–6, fills an important site adjoining Framwellgate Bridge with tact and ingenuity.

The biggest headache today, however, for every town, great or small, is how best to cope with the cars and the lorries. Durham had the good sense to enlist the services of an outstanding planner, Dr Thomas Sharp (1901–78), a native of the county.

47 (top).
Trevelyan College
48 (above).
Collingwood College

Until 1975 all the east-west traffic had to cross Elvet Bridge, climb steeply up to the Market Place, then drop precipitously down the equally narrow Silver Street to Framwellgate Bridge on the west side. It was a nightmare alike for the town and for the vehicles. In that year a new road was opened across the neck of the peninsula, *in a cutting*, and the river was crossed by two wide new bridges. The idea was Sharp's, conceived as early as 1945. It took thirty years to realise it, but at long last this was done. It is a brilliant piece of planning, which has been a boon to drivers and has enabled most of the old route to become pedestrianised. There is of course still far too much traffic for comfort, and no doubt there always will be, but I know of few towns that have solved this problem as successfully as Durham. In extensive areas of the town, and not only on the Rock, most people are not plagued by traffic any longer.

Scenically the town's greatest asset is no doubt its hilliness. The very steep hills, which pose such problems for lorries, have meant that some of the houses are quite dramatically placed. That is why the siting of every new building here has to be most carefully considered, as that of the National Savings Bank building certainly was not. Only the most exacting standards will suffice. For at Durham nothing, absolutely and positively nothing, must ever be permitted to intrude upon the great views. They are a priceless asset to the town, but they are much more: they belong to England – even, perhaps it should be said, to the whole world.

INDEX